Beat *the* Budget

CW00547118

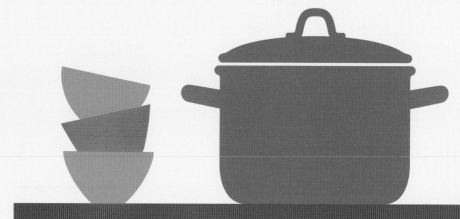

Mimi Harrison

Beat *the* Budget

Affordable easy recipes *and* simple meal prep

EBURY
PRESS

Contents

Introduction

Hello! I'm so glad you're here. Thank you for trusting me in the kitchen!

My name is Mimi and I'm the recipe developer, food blogger and photographer behind *Beat the Budget* – a platform where I share all kinds of easy, affordable and delicious recipes. Whatever you fancy, I have the budget answer without compromising on flavour!

I've always *loved* cooking. Both of my parents worked full-time, so from a young age my brother and I learnt to cook on our own. This started with a classic ready-made pesto pasta, but eventually grew into more of a passion as I became confident enough to experiment with flavour combinations and get more creative.

However, when I went to university, my enthusiasm for cooking hit a huge hurdle. I quickly realised that my £20 weekly budget couldn't cover the foods I was enjoying with my family at home. I wasn't able to afford my usual healthy and vibrant ingredients, so instead traded my protein and greens for cheesy chips and gravy. Although delicious for a while (and yes, I still adore a late-night cheesy chip!), by my third year I was really struggling – I wasn't enjoying food and I really didn't feel my best. I wanted to change up my diet and get back into cooking and enjoying meals that were tasty and affordable. I began planning my weekly shop, listing every ingredient and ensuring that nothing would go to waste. I created recipes where ingredients would overlap in order to bring down my total spend.

It took a bit of planning, but it wasn't long before I was back in the kitchen and eating well again. With a whole collection of recipes I'd built up to choose from, I realised just how easy it could be to stay within budget and eat feel-good food. As I listened to friends, it became clear that I wasn't the only one struggling with the cost of food, so I decided to start sharing my recipe ideas and advice online.

Fast forward four years and Beat the Budget has grown in ways that I could have only dreamed of – having this book out in the world is one of my biggest dreams and I still can't believe it came true. It's so satisfying seeing people make my recipes and knowing that I've been able to take the pressure off in some small way.

I'm so proud of this book and I can't wait for you guys to dive in. My hope is that it will help you to save money, stress less and highlight how easy it can be to eat yummy food on a budget.

Mimi x

Top Tips for Budgeting

Plan, Plan, Plan

It all comes down to planning. Spending around 20 minutes before you go shopping, checking what you need and writing a list will cut your costs massively. Oh, and don't go shopping on an empty stomach! A hangry brain will throw all sorts into the trolley. I break my shopping list into categories: Fresh (fruit, veg and herbs), Dairy, Meat & Seafood, Pantry, Frozen, and Cupboard Essentials. By grouping items in categories, you're not only saving time but you're preventing yourself from walking back and forth in store – which is what often leads to impulse buys en route. At the back of the book (pages 231–5) I've included five suggested menus with ingredients lists to get you started, which you can use to take the stress out of planning on a budget.

Cross-over Ingredients

I talk about cross-over ingredients a lot as it's one of the easiest ways to get the most out of your budget without feeling like you're having to compromise. I think of these as something that feature in multiple recipes, reducing waste and cutting costs. The trick here is to choose recipes where the cross-over ingredients don't feel repetitive. For example, you could use a pot of crème fraîche in a creamy pasta dish (Pork Stroganoff Orzo, see page 86) or risotto (Creamy Sun-dried Tomato & Pork Risotto, see page 146), drizzle it over fajitas or serve as a topping for soup. Each recipe feels completely different, whilst making the most of the same ingredient. When looking for recipes to pair together, think about ingredients that would cost more than one pound and see if you can find another recipe that can share the cost of that ingredient (for example, frozen bags of meat, cream, cheeses, vegetables, etc).

Love Your Freezer

If Gordon Ramsay has made you fear frozen food, I'm here to tell you otherwise. Not only is it a huge component that makes meal prep so successful (we'll get there later), but bulk-buying frozen ingredients in most cases cuts costs and reduces waste as you can simply defrost what you need whenever you need it (it often saves prep time, too). The amazing bonus is that freezing actually preserves nutrients, making frozen foods just as nutritious as their fresh competitors. I suggest experimenting and choosing your favourites – I love bulk buying frozen spinach as it's so much more affordable than fresh. I use it in warm recipes, adding a little spinach cube to individual portions as a 'nutrient bomb'. Get creative, find the frozen ingredients that work best for you and stock up. Freezing is also a helpful component of meal prep. Look out for the freezer icon to see which recipes you can freeze.

Shopping Around

Everyone has their favourite place to shop, but you can save money by doing a little research first. Find out which stores sell which products for the cheapest price. It may be that you buy two-thirds of your shop in one supermarket, then get branded goods or special deals in another. It can take a bit of planning, but with online shopping you can check prices from the comfort of your own home. Try to do one big, planned shop every week if you can, as this is the most economical way to shop.

Bulk Buying

Bulk buying is a fantastic way to keep your monthly food costs down. Consider purchasing dry or staple cupboard ingredients that have a naturally long shelf life in large amounts, like spices, oils, pasta, rice and those essentials listed on page 11. When it comes to bulk-buying fresh, always remember to check if the ingredient can be frozen. If it's too large to consume within a week (like a large bag of Cheddar, for example) you could freeze half when you get home and defrost for use when you need it. If you're unsure whether an item is suitable for freezing, do a quick 'search' on your phone in the supermarket, then you can work out if it's a good-value purchase.
I love buying big value bags of frozen veg as they have a much longer use-by date and are often already portioned into suitable sizes. Check out what's available in your local supermarket – you can often get great deals on frozen meat, too.

Meal Prep

Last but certainly not least, one of the most important tools in beating the budget is meal prep. Cooking recipes in batches of four, five or six portions, uses up ingredients, lowers waste and saves time – it also reduces energy costs as you're doing the bulk of the cooking in one session! A common mistake people often make with meal prep is trying to do it for every meal, seven days a week. This can get overwhelming – I recommend meal prepping for a maximum of four meals a week. This ensures you're reducing costs without restricting yourself so much that you give up on it completely. Meal prep doesn't mean you have to eat the same food every day. Choose a variety of recipes, then implement what I call a 'freezer cycle'; this is where you prep a different recipe (say five portions of each) three times a week. Place two portions in the fridge and three in the freezer (look out for the freezer icon). If you are using frozen ingredients, remember to check the packet instructions before adding to your freezer cycle. Some manufacturers do not advise re-freezing items once they have been defrosted. You can grab an individual serving whenever you fancy and after just a couple of weeks, you'll have a variety of recipes to choose from. If you're cooking for a family, you can double the recipes to maximise cost savings.

Cupboard Essentials

You don't need to be well-stocked in obscure ingredients to make my recipes as I've created every single dish using ingredients that are easy to find in your local supermarket. I've kept things simple, but there are some basics that I recommend you stock up on when you can to really make every meal you cook as tasty as possible. These cupboard essentials will last a lot longer than fresh ingredients, so although you might need to spend a bit more initially, they will last so you won't need to stock up again for a while.

I recommend three types of oils for best results at different heats – olive oil for general cooking over a medium heat, rapeseed oil for cooking over a high heat and extra virgin olive oil for salads and dressings or used over a low heat.

General

- Baking powder ☐
- Brown sugar ☐
- Cornflour ☐
- Dijon mustard ☐
- Flaky salt ☐
- Garlic powder ☐
- Honey ☐
- Ketchup (tomato) ☐
- Maple syrup ☐
  (substitute with honey if necessary)
- Mayonnaise ☐
- Onion powder ☐
- Peanut butter ☐
- Pepper (black) ☐
- Plain flour ☐
- Protein powder ☐
  (optional)
- Table salt ☐
- Soy sauce ☐
- Stock cubes ☐
- Tomato purée ☐
- Vanilla extract ☐

Spices

- Cayenne pepper ☐
- Chilli flakes ☐
- Cinnamon ☐
- Cumin ☐
- Curry powder ☐
- Garam masala ☐
- Paprika ☐
- Red pepper flakes ☐
- Smoked paprika ☐
- Turmeric ☐

Dried Herbs

- Dried basil ☐
- Dried oregano ☐
- Dried parsley ☐
- Dried thyme ☐
- Italian seasoning ☐

Vinegars

- Red wine vinegar ☐
- Rice vinegar ☐
- White wine vinegar ☐

Oils

- Extra virgin olive oil ☐
- Olive oil ☐
- Rapeseed oil ☐

How This Book Works

When I was deciding how to separate the chapters for the book, I came up with the idea that each section could provide ways to make meal times more exciting, whilst still being simple to prep and entirely affordable on a budget.

The Breakfast chapter features my go-to morning recipes to make the first meal of the day a bit more special. Forget expensive weekend brunches at restaurants – why not whip up some Sausage & Egg Muffins (see page 21) or my Healthy French Toast with Cinnamon (see page 27). Meal prep ahead for busy weekday mornings with my Loaded Pepper Shakshuka (see page 22) or a grab-and-go Spinach & Feta Frittata (see page 18).

In Soups, Salads & Sides I've tried to showcase tasty recipes that are stars in their own right and could be enjoyed at lunch or as an accompaniment to a main course when cooking for friends and family. A Halloumi Nourish Bowl (see page 60) makes a gorgeous, nutritious lunch or dinner for friends, and my Broccoli & Cheddar Soup with Jalapeños (see page 36) really spices up a quick meal on-the-go and freezes beautifully.

Weeknight Winners is packed full of delicious recipes, many of which can be made in under 30 minutes of preparation and cook time, so after a long day at work you can whip up a speedy, delicious pasta dish with a twist, like my Harissa Yoghurt Orzo (see page 88), or my Saag Paneer with Rice & Naan (see page 104), a warming curry that comes together in around 20 minutes.

I love opting for One-Pot Wonders when I'm not in the mood for cleaning as you only have to worry about washing up one pot. With minimal prep, my comforting Ginger & Lime Chicken Legs with Coconut Rice (see page 142) will make your kitchen smell divine, but can also be meal prepped ahead if you're short on time.

15 Minutes or Less is exactly what it says on the tin – express recipes for when you've had a crazy day and need a food fix, fast. Cacio e Pepe Gnocchi (see page 163) is a comforting spin on a classic dish with a more luxurious taste than the sum of its parts. Or a Fish Finger Burrito (see page 166) will almost certainly hit the spot for a speedy lunch or dinner.

The Fakeaways chapter features fan favourites from my blog and budget-friendly versions of all your favourite takeaways. From Peri-Peri Chicken Thighs (see page 204) to a Prawn Firecracker Curry (see page 200), there's a Friday night fakeaway recipe that will save you money and taste even more delicious than its takeaway version, I guarantee!

Last but not least the Sweet chapter includes cakes and desserts that are quick-to-prep crowd-pleasers, decadent enough to elevate the end of any meal. Dig into a Loaded Speculoos Banana Split (see page 219) or freeze a batch of my No-churn Salted Caramel Ice Cream (see page 222) to enjoy whenever it takes your fancy!

Cost Per Portion

I create all of my recipes with the aim of feeding 4–6 people for £1.25 a portion or less. It was so important for me to keep a strict limit to the cost per portion for every recipe so that you know exactly how much you're spending.

The Fakeaways chapter is the only section of the book where the budget is slightly higher, to give you maximum restaurant vibes from the comfort of your sofa. The maximum cost per serving is £1.55 (with the lowest cost in this section at just 11p), but you're still guaranteed to have delicious food that's a fraction of the price of ordering it in.

Meal Prep & Equipment

I have included tips to meal prep many of the dishes, so that they are suitable for families, individuals, couples and students. You can serve the full recipe or store portions for later depending on how many people you are catering for. Another cost-saving factor considered throughout the book is the use of energy-saving appliances. Due to skyrocketing energy prices, I thought it was necessary to consider oven and gas usage where appropriate and to offer further energy savings by using an air fryer, slow cooker or microwave when possible. Look out for these symbols to help you choose what to make ahead and how to cook it.

Tags & Nutritional Values

I wanted to make it super easy to identify suitable recipes at-a-glance by including dietary tags. Look out for veggie, vegan, high protein, dairy-free, gluten-free, low-fat and low-carb tags, so you can easily pick and choose which dishes will suit you or your friends and family. For those who track their macros and calories, I have created a nutritional value table listing each recipe. The table is organised by chapter and can be found on my website through the QR code above. You can search for your chosen recipes and get those tracked. Recipes that can be frozen should keep for to three months and be defrosted in the fridge overnight before properly heated, unless otherwise stated in the recipe notes.

Breakfast

```
- - - - - - - - - - - - - - - - - - - - - - - - - - - -

Creamy Mushroom Toast                    16

Spinach & Feta Frittata                  18

Sausage & Egg Muffins                    21

Loaded Pepper Shakshuka                  22

Boujee Budget Brunch                     24

Healthy French Toast                     27
with Cinnamon

Healthy Banana Blueberry Muffins         28

Raspberry Pancakes                       30

Chocolate Hazelnut Baked Oats            33


- - - - - - - - - - - - - - - - - - - - - - - - - - - -
```

Creamy Mushroom Toast

5 min prep + 8 min cook

This dish is 'more than the sum of its parts'. With a few ingredients and ten minutes of your time, you get the most delicious breakfast that's packed full of flavour. Browned soy-saucy mushrooms and cream cheese may seem like an odd combo but trust me on this one – the salty, buttery, umami-packed mushrooms contrast perfectly with the comforting layer of cream cheese. The rocket adds both nutrients and a peppery flavour which makes this one of my fave breakfasts. Don't hold back on the black pepper as generous seasoning will make this dish sing.

Serves 1

1½ tbsp salted butter
1 slice sourdough
½ tbsp rapeseed oil
handful of mushrooms
   (I used shiitake)
1 tsp soy sauce
1 garlic clove, crushed
2 tbsp low-fat cream cheese
handful of rocket
juice of ¼ lemon
salt and pepper to taste
pinch of chilli flakes (optional)

1. Lightly butter both sides of the sourdough with half a tablespoon of butter and fry over a high heat for one minute on each side until toasted. Remove from the pan and keep warm

2. Next, add the rapeseed oil and mushrooms to the pan. Spread out so they aren't touching. Leave to brown over a high heat for a couple of minutes, then stir.

3. Reduce the heat and add the soy sauce, the remaining one tablespoon of butter and the garlic. Season with salt and lots of pepper and fry for a couple more minutes. Set the mushroom mix aside.

4. Spread a layer of cream cheese onto your crispy toast, add the rocket and then spoon over the saucy, browned mushrooms. Add the lemon juice and a pinch of chilli flakes, if you like.

Spinach & Feta Frittata

Freeze Gluten Free Low Carb Veggie High Protein

5 min prep + 15 min cook

Note: *If you use normal spinach (often cheaper than baby spinach!), roughly chop the leaves a little before adding to the pan so that the pieces aren't too big. Any variety of tomato will work in this recipe, just be sure to thinly slice before adding to the frittata mix.*

This recipe is one that looks and tastes like you've put a lot of effort in, without actually having to do much work. Tangy and rich feta cheese pairs perfectly with the slight bitterness of spinach, and it's so reasonably priced when compared to other cheeses. This could be a Sunday brunch feast to enjoy with family and friends or you could serve it as a meal prep dish – why not whip this recipe up on a Monday morning and enjoy individual breakfast servings throughout the week?

Serves 5

1 tbsp olive oil
50 g spring onions, thinly sliced
12 eggs
75 ml milk
3 garlic cloves, crushed
240 g baby spinach, rinsed and dried
100 g feta cheese
250 g cherry tomatoes, thinly sliced
salt and pepper to taste
small handful of fresh dill, roughly torn

1. Preheat the oven to 210°C/190°C Fan.

2. Add the olive oil to a large, oven-safe frying pan and set over a medium/low heat. Add the spring onions (reserving some for garnish) and fry for a few minutes. Season with salt and lots of pepper.

3. Meanwhile, add the eggs to a large bowl and pour in the milk, whisking continuously to combine. Season with salt and pepper.

4. Add the garlic and spinach to the spring onions in the pan. Cook for about a minute until the spinach has wilted down.

5. Pour the egg mix into the pan. Crumble the feta over the egg/ spinach mix, spreading the pieces evenly across the pan. Scatter about one-third of the cherry tomatoes over the egg mix, reserving the remaining two-thirds to enjoy fresh when serving.

6. Place the pan in the oven for 8–10 minutes, or until the egg is just firm and cooked. Check at the 8-minute mark and be quick to remove the pan (safely!) as soon as the egg has firmed, so that the frittata doesn't dry out.

7. Garnish with fresh dill, the reserved spring onions and a grind of black pepper. Serve with the remaining slices of cherry tomatoes on the side and dig in!

Meal Prep

Store the garnish (fresh dill, sliced tomatoes and spring onion) separately in the fridge and keep the cooked frittata in a sealed container in the fridge for up to four days. When it's time to eat, either enjoy cold or reheat in a non-stick frying pan over a medium heat for two minutes, or until hot through.

Sausage & Egg Muffins

Freeze

5 min prep + 20 min cook

Note: *If you have a muffin tin, divide the egg mix between four of the holes. Bake for five minutes at 180°C/160°C Fan. If you only have a frying pan, set to a medium heat and add the egg mix to the pan. Cook until firm (like an omelette) and cut into individual portions to serve.*

Serves 4

450 g (about 8) sausages
6 large eggs
50 g spring onions, thinly sliced
1 tbsp rapeseed oil
4 English muffins, halved and toasted
4 cheese slices
1 tbsp mayonnaise (optional)
salt and pepper to taste

This is inspired by one of my favourite fast-food breakfasts. It's so satisfying and flavourful and you won't have the hidden extra costs of a takeaway or the waiting time! The eggs have been boujee-fied with the addition of spring onion and I like that the rich flavour of the yolk is incorporated throughout the whisked egg patty which takes this recipe to the next level. In under 20 minutes you could be enjoying the most delicious breakfast muffin, so what are you waiting for?

1. Start by removing the sausage meat, squeezing it out of the sausage casing and forming it into four equal-sized balls. Flatten and shape the balls into burger shapes and set to one side.

2. In a large mixing bowl, whisk the eggs together with the spring onions. Season with salt and pepper.

3. Set a non-stick frying pan over a high heat and add the rapeseed oil. Once the pan is hot, add the burgers to the pan (fry in two batches if your pan is too small to fit all four at once). Fry for three minutes on each side until nicely browned and cooked through. Set aside and keep warm.

4. To the same pan, add a cookie cutter or egg mould, set over a medium heat and carefully pour in a serving of the egg mix. Cook for around two minutes, or until the egg has firmed up. Meanwhile, add the bottom halves of the toasted muffins to the pan and layer a cheese slice on each piece. Cover with a lid to allow the cheese to melt slightly for a few minutes. Repeat this process until all the muffins are ready.

5. To serve, assemble a muffin by placing one half of the cheesy muffin on a plate, adding the burger on top. Next, remove the cooked egg from the cookie cutter or mould and layer over the burger. Add a thin layer of mayonnaise if you prefer, followed by the final muffin half to finish. Repeat to make the remaining muffins.

Meal Prep

Follow steps 1-5, then wrap tightly in cling film and foil. Freeze for up to a month. When it's time to eat, remove the casing and wrap in a paper towel. Reheat in the microwave on high for two minutes, or until hot.

Loaded Pepper Shakshuka

Low Carb

5 min prep + 25 min cook

Note: *Defrost the frozen peppers overnight in the fridge or in your microwave for five minutes, set to defrost. Be sure to drain the peppers of their excess liquid before adding to the pan.*

Shakshuka is one of my favourite one-pot breakfast recipes. It is a Tunisian dish, with the word 'shakshuka' translating to 'all mixed up'. I've added looooots of peppers to my version which isn't traditional. However, I think the mixed peppers pair amazingly with the smoky flavours of the sauce. Plus, using a large frozen bag of peppers is not only cheaper than fresh, but it reduces the prep time significantly. A cheap alternative to fresh garlic is a jar of chopped garlic that you can store in the fridge for a long time and use for multiple recipes. The bonus being that you don't even have to prepare the garlic yourself!

Serves 5

1 tbsp olive oil
200 g smoked bacon lardons
1 onion, thinly sliced
3 garlic cloves, crushed
2 tsp paprika
600 g frozen peppers, defrosted and excess liquid drained
2 x 400 g cans chopped tomatoes
1 tsp honey
5 large eggs
salt and pepper to taste
large handful of fresh parsley, leaves torn
pinch of chilli flakes (optional)
crusty bread loaf, torn into pieces

1. Set a wide, deep frying pan over a medium/low heat, add the olive oil and lardons and fry for five minutes.

2. Add the onion to the pan and season with salt and pepper. Continue to fry for about four minutes, or until softened. Add the garlic and paprika for the final minute of frying time.

3. Add the peppers to the pan and increase the heat. Cook until any moisture is fully released and cooked off. This will take about eight minutes.

4. Pour the chopped tomatoes into the pan along with the honey. Stir to combine, reduce the heat to medium and season with salt and pepper.

5. Use a spoon to form five little wells in the mixture and crack an egg into each one, ensuring they are well spaced out. Season the eggs with salt and pepper and cover with a lid for 7–8 minutes to cook.

6. Garnish with fresh parsley and chilli flakes if you like the heat. Serve with pieces of crusty bread on the side for dipping!

Meal Prep

Cook the tomato sauce ahead of time, following steps 1-4. Store in the fridge for up to three days. When it's time to eat, add the tomato sauce to a frying pan over a medium heat, follow steps 5-6 and tuck in! Check your pack of frozen vegetables for heating instructions, as some manufacturers do not recommend reheating their products.

Boujee Budget Brunch

5 min prep + 30 min cook

Note: *You can substitute standard button mushrooms or chestnut mushrooms to make this recipe even cheaper. Slice them in half to prep and follow the same method.*

This is the ideal recipe for a lazy Sunday, when you want to save money on that hangover breakfast without sacrificing the indulgence of a boujee brunch. Avocado toast on a budget? Yes please! This dish is loaded with vegetarian-friendly ingredients so you'll definitely be able to include everyone in this feast. If you are dining with vegans, substitute the crumbled feta for green olives and the honey for maple syrup.

Serves 5

250 g portobello mushrooms
250 g cherry tomatoes
3 tbsp extra virgin olive oil
drizzle of soy sauce
2 x 240 g cans mixed beans, drained and rinsed
1 x 400 g can chopped tomatoes
1 tsp paprika
1 tsp ground cumin
1 tsp honey
5 slices seeded bread, toasted
2 avocados, sliced
200 g feta cheese, crumbled to serve
large handful of fresh parsley, torn to serve
salt and pepper to taste
pinch of chilli flakes (optional)

1. Preheat the oven to 200°C/180°C Fan.

2. Add the mushrooms to a baking dish and the cherry tomatoes to another. Pour one tablespoon of olive oil into each dish and season with salt and pepper, stirring to coat the vegetables. Arrange the mushrooms with their tops facing down to allow any moisture to seep out.

3. Transfer both dishes to the oven and cook for 15 minutes. Remove from the oven, shake the tomatoes and rotate the mushrooms, drizzling a little soy sauce over the mushrooms before returning both dishes to the oven for another 15 minutes.

4. Meanwhile, add the mixed beans and chopped tomatoes to a medium pan. Fill the empty tomato can with water and pour into the pan.

5. Add the paprika, cumin, honey and a grind of salt and pepper to the pan. Increase the heat to medium/high and simmer for 12 minutes. The boujee bean mix should be thick, yet saucy when ready.

6. To serve, top each slice of toasted bread with a drizzle of the remaining olive oil, some avocado slices and salt and pepper to taste. Add a portobello mushroom, a spoonful of juicy tomatoes and a generous helping of boujee beans. Sprinkle the feta and parsley over and, if you love a bit of heat, add a pinch of chilli flakes, too.

Healthy French Toast with Cinnamon

Veggie

5 min prep + 25 min cook

I like to think of this recipe as a healthy fakeaway answer to an American diner-style breakfast. The crispy pan-fried cinnamon toast is sweet enough to feel like dessert, but warming enough to fuel a great breakfast. Buying frozen mixed berries keeps the recipe within budget as the same variety of fresh mixed berries would cost much more. I also love that when the berries start to defrost, they become super juicy and their jewel-like colours mix with the thick Greek yoghurt. It's the perfect way to start your day.

Serves 4

8 thick slices wholemeal bread
100 g frozen mixed berries
3 eggs
100 ml skimmed milk
1 tsp vanilla extract
2 tbsp honey, plus extra to serve
1 tsp ground cinnamon, plus
    extra to serve
2 tbsp olive oil
4 tbsp 0% fat Greek yoghurt

1. If possible, leave the slices of bread on a baking sheet, uncovered overnight to dry out before cooking. Defrost the frozen mixed berries overnight in the fridge, otherwise microwave for 30-second intervals on a defrost setting until no longer frozen.

2. Whisk together the eggs, milk, vanilla extract, honey and cinnamon in a bowl until combined.

3. Add half a tablespoon of the olive oil to a large, non-stick frying pan over a medium heat. Dunk two stale slices of bread into the egg mix and transfer to the hot pan.

4. After around three minutes, or when golden, flip and repeat the process on the other side. Transfer to a low oven to keep warm and continue dunking and frying the remaining slices, using half a tablespoon of oil for each batch.

5. Serve the French toast with a dollop of Greek yoghurt, a handful of mixed berries, a squeeze of honey and an extra sprinkle of cinnamon.

Air Fryer
Follow steps 1-3. Grease the basket with a few sprays of oil and place in the air fryer, preheated to 190°C, for five minutes.

Healthy Banana Blueberry Muffins

15 min prep + 25 min cook

Note: *Overmixing can result in a tough dense muffin, so be sure to only mix until just combined.*

There are a few ingredients that I believe a breakfast muffin needs in order to start your day. Firstly, they should be packed with fruit, preferably two types to maximise nutrients and flavour. Next, they have to be large enough to fill you up as the first meal of the day. Finally, they need to be tasty. For me, this breakfast bake ticks all the boxes. The addition of banana gives a deliciously moist yet light muffin with bursts of berry flavour throughout. Make a batch to eat throughout the week so that you can grab breakfast on the go.

Makes 8

3 tbsp coconut oil, melted,
   plus extra for greasing
340 g plain flour, sifted
3 tsp baking powder
½ tsp ground cinnamon
¼ tsp salt
3 bananas, peeled
1 large egg
4 tbsp honey
60 g natural yoghurt
1 tsp vanilla extract
275 ml milk
175 g frozen blueberries
brown sugar (optional)

1. Preheat the oven to 240°C/220°C Fan. Grease an eight-hole muffin tin with a little coconut oil.

2. First, combine the dry ingredients. Add the flour, baking powder, cinnamon and salt to a bowl and stir until combined.

3. In a separate bowl, add the bananas and mash them well with a fork. Add the melted coconut oil and egg and stir. Then add the honey, yoghurt, vanilla extract and milk and whisk until combined.

4. Gradually add the dry ingredients to the wet ingredients, folding gently and continuously to keep air in the mix. When just combined, fold the frozen blueberries into the mix and then divide equally between the holes of the prepared muffin tin, filling each to the top. Sprinkle brown sugar over each muffin if you prefer a crunchy top!

5. Place the muffin tin in the oven and bake for five minutes, then reduce the temperature to 200°C/180°C Fan (without opening the door!) and bake for a further 20 minutes.

Raspberry Pancakes

Low Fat   Veggie

5 min prep + 25 min cook

These fluffy American-inspired pancakes are the perfect balanced breakfast. The batter comes together in one bowl, and these are so, so tasty. I've used frozen raspberries to ensure that this recipe can be made all year round and it also reduces costs. I find that fresh raspberries go off really quickly, so substituting for frozen is always a great shout when cooking.

Makes 20

300 g self-raising flour, sifted
1½ tsp baking powder
2 large eggs
5 tbsp honey, plus extra to drizzle
150 g natural yoghurt
150 ml milk
1 tsp vanilla extract
2 tbsp rapeseed oil
150 g frozen raspberries,
  defrosted

1. Add the flour and baking powder to a large bowl and stir to combine.

2. Take a separate bowl and whisk together the eggs, honey, yoghurt, milk and vanilla extract. Slowly pour the wet mix into the flour mix, whisking continuously until a smooth consistency is achieved.

3. Lightly brush a non-stick frying pan with a little of the rapeseed oil and set over a medium heat. When the pan is hot, add about two tablespoons/one large spoonful of the pancake batter to make one pancake. You should be able to fit about three pancakes in the pan at one time.

4. Break up the raspberries so they are in pieces and scatter a few over each pancake. When the bottom of each pancake starts to turn golden, flip them and cook for a further few minutes.

5. Serve the pancakes stacked high, with the remaining raspberries scattered over to decorate and a drizzle of honey.

Chocolate Hazelnut Baked Oats

Veggie

3 min prep + 12 min cook

Note: *Cooking time will depend on the size of your ramekin, so adjust as necessary.*

If you wake up craving something sweet, why not try this breakfast variation of a molten lava cake to start the day? The baked oat base is made from staple store-cupboard essentials. When heated, the chocolate hazelnut spread melts into the best gooey, nutty, chocolatey centre that will guarantee an easier wake-up on Monday morning or a luxurious weekend treat. If you have protein powder in the cupboard, you can add a scoop at the blending stage for an extra protein boost. I opted for chocolate protein powder here for an extra chocolatey hit.

Serves 1

1 tsp butter (for greasing)
50 g oats
100 ml oat milk or milk of choice
1 scoop protein powder (optional)
1 egg
1 tsp honey or soft brown sugar (optional)
½ tsp baking powder
½ tbsp chocolate hazelnut spread
1 tbsp milk chocolate chips

1. Preheat the oven to 195°C/175°C Fan. Grease a 15 cm ramekin lightly with butter.

2. Combine the oats, oat milk, protein powder (if using), egg, honey and baking powder in a blender and blitz until smooth.

3. Pour half the blended mix into the prepared ramekin. Add the chocolate hazelnut spread to the centre and distribute slightly with a spoon to ensure it will be submerged. Then pour over the remaining blended mix.

4. Sprinkle over the chocolate chips. Pop in the oven for 12 minutes and enjoy!

Soups, Salads & Sides

Broccoli & Cheddar Soup with Jalapeños

Freeze • High Protein • Veggie

7 min prep + 25 min cook

Everyone loves this soup and it's one of my favourite ways to enjoy broccoli. So, when I had the idea to add the best tangy, spicy topping (hello, jalapeños!), I had high hopes and it turned out to be a dream combo. The soup itself is hearty and warming, but the spice cuts through and every mouthful tastes vibrant and bright. It keeps well in the freezer and fridge, so it could be an easy work-from-home lunch or a meal on-the-go if you have access to a microwave. The optional side of cheese on toast uses the same block of Cheddar that is used in the soup, so it's within budget while also being the ultimate vehicle to scoop your soup up with.

Serves 5

1 tbsp olive oil
1 onion, diced
2 heads of broccoli, separated into florets, stalks finely chopped
3–4 garlic cloves, crushed
3–5 tbsp pickled jalapeños, roughly chopped +1 tbsp brine
900 ml vegetable stock
small loaf crusty bread, sliced (optional)
300–400 g Cheddar, grated
400 ml milk
large handful of fresh parsley or chives, roughly chopped
salt and pepper to taste

1. Preheat the grill to medium (if you plan to serve the soup with a side of cheese on toast).

2. Set a large pan over a medium heat and add the olive oil, onion and the finely chopped broccoli stalks. Season with salt and pepper and fry for eight minutes.

3. Next, add the garlic and jalapeños to fry for a minute before adding the florets and the vegetable stock. Bring to a low simmer and cook for 15 minutes.

4. Meanwhile, prepare the cheese on toast. Sprinkle some grated cheese over slices of crusty bread and place under the grill for about six minutes, or until the bread is toasted and the cheese is melted.

5. Stir the milk, 150 g of Cheddar and the jalapeño brine into the large pan and blitz until smooth using a stick blender.

6. Serve each portion of soup with a sprinkle of extra cheese, jalapeños, a generous crack of black pepper and a side of cheese on toast for dunking.

Meal Prep Simply chill a batch of soup in the fridge for up to three days and microwave on high for two minutes to reheat. Or store in the freezer for up to three months and defrost in the fridge overnight before reheating. Always make the cheese on toast fresh.

Slow Cooker Chicken with Nduja Brothy Beans

Slow Cooker · **Freeze** · **Dairy Free** · **High Protein**

5-10 min prep + 3-5 hr cook

Note: *To make without a slow cooker: Add 1 tbsp of olive oil and onion to a large saucepan, season with salt and fry for around 4 minutes. Add the garlic and nduja and fry for a minute or until fragrant. Then throw all the ingredients into the pan (except the kale) and gently simmer for 45 minutes. Cover with a lid. Add the kale for the final two minutes of cook time, then follow steps 3–4.*

If you want a recipe that requires the least amount of effort, with the most amount of flavour, look no further. Italian nduja paste is a spreadable sausage paste infused with Calabrian chillies which imparts a rich, savoury flavour to the broth and makes this meal so comforting and warming. It requires less than ten minutes of prep and the slow cooker does the rest of the work for you. I opt for on the bone, skin-on chicken thighs as these are the most affordable cut - plus the extra flavour you get from the bones and skin is such a bonus. The use of dried beans instead of canned is highly recommended here as when they're slow cooked, the flavour and texture is so, so good. For a thicker soup, opt for 500 g dried white beans or for a thinner broth, use 400 g. Dried beans absorb a lot of moisture as they cook. If using canned white beans, the chicken stock should be reduced to 1.4 litres, as canned beans don't absorb as much liquid.

Serves 6

1.1 kg chicken thighs, skin on, on the bone
4 tbsp nduja paste
4 garlic cloves, crushed
1 red onion, sliced into thin wedges
2 litres chicken stock
5 sprigs of fresh rosemary
400–500 g dried white beans
150 g kale, washed, stems removed and leaves torn
salt and pepper to taste
pinch of chilli flakes (optional)

1. Set a large frying pan over a medium heat and fry the chicken thighs until the skin is golden and crisp. No oil is needed here as the chicken fat will render. You could miss this step out, but it does maximise flavour.

2. Add the chicken thighs (and the rendered fat left in the pan) to the slow cooker. Add the nduja, garlic, red onion, chicken stock, rosemary and beans. Season with salt and pepper and stir to combine. Cook on low for 4–5 hours, or on high for three hours. When almost ready, stir the kale into the broth to wilt for ten minutes.

3. Just before serving, remove the chicken thighs from the broth, remove the skin and discard and tear the juicy chicken meat from the bone, returning the meat back to the broth and discarding the bones.

4. Serve with lots of black pepper and add chilli flakes, if you like.

Meal Prep

Divide the cooked broth into portions and store in the fridge for up to four days. Store in the freezer for up to three months and defrost in the fridge overnight. As the beans absorb liquid during storage, add 100 ml of water before reheating each portion in the microwave on high for two minutes. Season with salt and pepper.

French Onion Soup

5 min prep + 45 min cook

I've taken the much-loved French onion soup and made some switches to make it more affordable. Traditionally, French onion soup uses Gruyère and white wine, but I opt for Gouda as a deliciously cheaper alternative. White wine is subbed for red wine vinegar so that you don't have to give up a precious glass or two at dinner. The result is a rich and deeply savoury soup that is perfect for a cosy night in. I've also adapted the cooking method to use less energy, to further reduce the cost per serving.

Serves 4

60 g butter
1 tbsp olive oil
4 onions, thinly sliced
1 tbsp honey
3 tbsp plain flour
3 garlic cloves, crushed
1.5 litres beef stock
1 tbsp soy sauce
1 tbsp red wine vinegar
8 sprigs of fresh thyme
200 g Gouda, grated
1 baguette, sliced into 2-cm
   rounds, toasted
salt and pepper to taste
handful of fresh chives, finely
   chopped

1. Preheat the oven to 220°C/200°C Fan.

2. Set a deep non-stick frying pan over a low/medium heat and add the butter and olive oil. Once the butter has melted, add the onions, generously season with salt and pepper and fry for 15 minutes.

3. Drizzle the honey into the pan and increase the heat slightly. Continue to fry for another 15 minutes, stirring occasionally until the onions are caramelised.

4. Add the flour to the pan and cook for a couple of minutes, along with the garlic before deglazing with a splash of the beef stock. Pour the rest of the beef stock into the pan, along with the soy sauce, red wine vinegar and thyme. Reduce the heat to a simmer for 15 minutes.

5. Meanwhile, sprinkle the Gouda over four toasted rounds of bread. Place on a baking sheet in the oven to bake until the cheese has melted.

6. Ladle a portion of the soup into each bowl. Top with a slice of the cheesy bread and garnish with some fresh chives.

Creamy Mushroom & Cashew Soup

Freeze   Vegan

5 min prep + 30 min cook

The creaminess of this soup makes it hard to believe that it's vegan and in my opinion it surpasses every other of my dairy-based mushroom soups. It also incorporates two ingredients that are packed full of umami flavour – mushrooms and soy sauce. These add a unique savoury depth of flavour that puts this soup at the top of my favourites list. There is nothing more comforting than a soup simmering away on the hob and when it's as delicious as this one, you'll be counting down the minutes until you can tuck in.

Serves 5

150 g raw cashews
2 tbsp rapeseed oil
750 g chestnut mushrooms,
   thinly sliced
2 onions, diced
3 garlic cloves, crushed
1–2 tbsp fresh thyme leaves, plus
   (optional) extra to garnish
1 litre vegetable stock
1½ tbsp soy sauce
150 ml water
juice of ½ lemon
salt and pepper to taste

1. Add the cashews to a heatproof bowl and cover with boiling water, ensuring that the cashews are submerged. Leave to soak until needed.

2. Set a large pan over a high heat, add one tablespoon of rapeseed oil and one-third of the mushrooms. Leave to brown for eight minutes, rotating once halfway through. Set the browned mushrooms aside.

3. Reduce the heat to medium and add the remaining rapeseed oil, the onions and remaining mushrooms to the pan. Season with salt and pepper and fry for seven minutes.

4. Next, add the garlic and thyme to fry for a minute before adding the vegetable stock and soy sauce. Bring to a low simmer for 12 minutes.

5. Meanwhile, make the cashew cream by adding the soaked (drained) cashews and the measured water to a blender and blitzing until smooth.

6. Use a stick blender to blitz the soup until smooth, then pour two-thirds of the cashew cream into the soup. Add the lemon juice, stir until combined and season with salt and pepper to taste.

7. Serve each portion of soup with a little swirl of the remaining cashew cream. Top with some reserved browned mushrooms and a grinding of black pepper. Sprinkle over some fresh thyme to garnish if you have any left.

Meal Prep

Add all the cashew cream to the soup when making this ahead of time. Store the soup in the fridge for up to three days and microwave on high for two minutes to reheat. Or store in the freezer for up to three months and defrost in the fridge overnight before reheating. Store the browned mushrooms separately in the fridge.

Soups, Salads & Sides

Slow Cooker Chorizo & Butter Bean Stew

Freeze · Slow Cooker · High Protein

5 min prep + 4 hr cook

Note: *To make without a slow cooker: Follow the same method using a deep saucepan. After all of the ingredients are added in step 4, simmer on low until the beans are soft and creamy.*

If you're looking for a meal that's comforting and packed with flavour, but requires minimal effort, stop and stew on this recipe. Thanks to my slow cooker, I can get on with the day while my dinner takes care of itself in the background. I very rarely call for any sort of dried bean in a recipe, as canned beans are a cheap and convenient ingredient. However, as this stew cooks slowly, I would advise using dried beans here. They give the creamiest, richest texture, which when served in a chorizo-infused tomato stew feels really special. If you still need persuading, slow cookers are super energy efficient, so you can make even more savings by cooking this recipe.

Serves 5

1 tbsp olive oil
225 g chorizo sausage, paper removed and chopped into chunks
1 onion, finely chopped
1 tbsp tomato purée
3 garlic cloves, crushed
2 tsp paprika
½ tsp cayenne pepper
1 x 400 g can chopped tomatoes
1.8 litres chicken stock
375 g dried butter beans
250 g cherry tomatoes, halved
180 g spinach
5 tbsp soured cream
large handful of chopped fresh chives
large handful of grated Cheddar (optional)

1. Pour the olive oil into a non-stick frying pan and place over a medium heat. Add the chorizo chunks to the pan and fry for about four minutes until slightly crispy.

2. Remove the chorizo with a slotted spoon and set aside, leaving all of the flavoured oil in the pan. Add the onion and sweat until soft.

3. Once softened, add the tomato purée, garlic, paprika and cayenne pepper to fry for one minute before transferring to the slow cooker.

4. Add the chopped tomatoes, chicken stock, butter beans, cherry tomatoes and fried chorizo chunks (reserving some for garnish). Stir to combine, set the slow cooker to high and cook for a minimum of three hours. Depending on how powerful your slow cooker is, it might take a bit longer. When the beans are soft and creamy, add the spinach to the pot to wilt in the residual heat and stir through.

5. Serve each bowl of stew with a tablespoon of soured cream, a few reserved chorizo chunks, a sprinkle of chives and a sprinkle of Cheddar, if you like. So, so good.

Panzanella Salad with Halloumi

5 min prep + 10 min cook

A cheese and bread salad – sounds like a good time, right? Panzanella salad is a Tuscan dish that involves using stale crusty bread which has been pan-fried to crisp it up, then mixing it with an array of fresh ingredients. Now when your ciabatta loaf has been left out and subsequently turned sad and dry looking, don't worry, it can be a happy occasion! The halloumi pieces (although inauthentic to a panzanella salad) act as a tangy, salty hit of flavour when combined with the other ingredients, making this the ultimate summer salad.

Serves 4

1 tsp + 2 tbsp rapeseed oil
225 g low fat halloumi cheese, sliced into thin squares
2 stale ciabatta rolls, about 180 g, sliced into large cubes
1 whole cucumber, sliced into half moons
½ red onion, thinly sliced
500 g cherry tomatoes, halved
1 tbsp red wine vinegar
2 tbsp extra virgin olive oil
salt and pepper to taste

1. Heat a non-stick frying pan over a medium heat, add one teaspoon of rapeseed oil and fry the halloumi until golden on both sides. Set aside.

2. To the same pan, add the ciabatta cubes along with the remaining two tablespoons of rapeseed oil. Fry over a medium heat until golden and crispy. Set aside to cool with the halloumi.

3. Add the sliced cucumber, onion and tomatoes to a large bowl, pour over the red wine vinegar and olive oil and stir to combine. Add the crispy bread cubes and halloumi squares, season with salt and pepper and stir together one last time. Enjoy!

Tortilla-crusted Chicken Caesar Salad

10 min prep + 10 min cook

Chicken Caesar always has been and always will be my favourite salad. It's creamy, crispy, tangy and refreshing - everything you could ask for in a salad. This recipe takes a simplified (with no flavours compromised) Caesar dressing, but instead of traditional crispy croutons, the chicken breast itself is battered in a tortilla crust. You can even adapt the batter by selecting your favourite tortilla chip flavour, whether that's original, tangy cheese or a spicy heat variety.

Serves 4

½ garlic clove, crushed
3 tbsp mayonnaise
1 tbsp Dijon mustard or wholegrain mustard
juice of ½ lemon, plus extra to serve
2 tbsp rapeseed oil + enough to coat the bottom of the pan
2 boneless, skinless chicken breasts, about 350 g total weight, sliced horizontally in half
2 tbsp plain flour
1–2 eggs, whisked
120 g tortilla chips, crushed to breadcrumb-like texture
2 heads of baby gem lettuce, leaves washed
50 g Parmesan, finely grated
salt and pepper to taste

1. Put the crushed garlic and a pinch of salt on a chopping board. Use the side of your knife to squish and drag the garlic across the board to form a garlic paste. The salt acts as an abrasive to help break it down, so make sure you add enough here!

2. Add the garlic paste to a mixing bowl with the mayonnaise, mustard and lemon juice. Season with plenty of black pepper and whisk to combine.

3. Slowly pour two tablespoons of rapeseed oil into the dressing, whisking continuously. Taste to check for seasoning and add salt and pepper if necessary. Set aside.

4. Pound the four chicken breast halves to ensure they are each roughly two centimetres thick. Add the flour to one plate, the whisked egg to a shallow bowl and the crushed tortilla chips to another plate.

5. Using one hand, coat the chicken evenly in the flour, then transfer to the whisked egg using your other hand and coat fully. Transfer to the tortilla plate and use your dry hand to scoop the crumbs over the chicken breast, patting them to help them stick. This double-handed method will stop the crumbs from sticking to your hands! Set each coated chicken breast to the side on a clean plate.

6. Set a non-stick frying pan over a medium heat, add rapeseed oil to a depth of about one centimetre and heat for two minutes, then add two chicken pieces at a time and fry for two minutes on each side, or until cooked. Remove from the pan and season immediately with salt and set aside. Repeat with the remaining two chicken breasts.

7. Either assemble as one large salad in a big bowl, or as single servings of salad in smaller bowls. Toss the lettuce in the dressing and arrange in the bowl(s). Slice the cooled, crispy chicken into bite-sized pieces and pile onto the lettuce. Top with the Parmesan and a squeeze of lemon juice.

Meal Prep

Assemble the dressing and store in a sealed container or jar in the fridge. Store the washed and dried lettuce leaves in a meal prep container lined with kitchen paper, spaced apart to prevent them from going soggy. When it's time to eat, proceed with steps 4-7. To ensure your chicken stays fresh, you could freeze half of the chicken pieces for later on in the week. Keep your packet of tortilla chips sealed when stored so they don't turn stale and to maximise crispiness when frying.

Chopped Mango Salad with a Creamy Basil Dressing

15 min prep

Take the green goddess chopped salad that went viral and add even more colour, a shorter ingredients list and a serving of fruit. The result is this deliciously crunchy lunch that you can scale up or down depending on the occasion. You can flex your knife skills with the chopping required (or take it slow and relax if you have none). It's such a nourishing, colourful bowl that really encourages you to 'eat the rainbow'. However, any salad that includes crisps as an ingredient is always a happy salad for me!

Serves 5

For the dressing
50 g raw cashews
30 g fresh basil
juice of ½ lime, plus wedges
  to serve
large pinch of salt
4 tbsp extra virgin olive oil
4 tbsp water

For the salad
1 red cabbage, finely chopped
1 mango, peeled, stoned and
  sliced into cubes
250 g cherry tomatoes, chopped
  into quarters
1 cucumber, diced
60 g rocket, roughly chopped
180 g tortilla chips

1. Put the cashews in a heatproof bowl and cover with enough boiling water to submerge them. If possible, soak for 30 minutes, but ten minutes minimum would also work if you're in a rush.

2. Meanwhile, use the soaking time to prepare your vegetables and fruit for the salad.

3. Take a large bowl and add the cabbage, mango, cherry tomatoes, cucumber and rocket. Set aside.

4. To a blender, add the soaked (drained) cashews, basil (including stems), lime juice, a large pinch of salt, the olive oil and water. Blitz until smooth to achieve a thick dressing. Pour the dressing over the chopped salad ingredients and stir to coat evenly.

5. Serve each portion of the chopped salad in a bowl with a serving of tortilla chips. Serve with a lime wedge. Switch up the scooping vehicle, using a fork or tortilla chip as you dig in!

Meal Prep

Store the prepped vegetables separately in sealed containers in the fridge to maximise freshness. Store the rocket in a container lined with kitchen paper to prevent it from going soggy. On the day that you're going to eat, blitz one (or more) serving of the dressing ingredients (you may need to add an extra splash of water to help blend) before drizzling over the assembled salad.

Soups, Salads & Sides

Kale Salad with Goats' Cheese & Roasted Butternut Squash

Gluten Free Veggie

10 min prep + 35 min cook

If you're sceptical about eating raw kale, this is the salad to convert you. By massaging the kale with olive oil and salt, the leaves are softened giving the most delicious autumnal salad base. The roasted paprika-infused butternut squash pairs perfectly with the tangy goats' cheese, while the creamy honey and mustard dressing takes this combo to the next level. If you want to reduce prep time and cost per head even further, purchase frozen cubed/peeled squash instead of fresh.

Serves 4

1 large butternut squash, peeled and cubed or sliced into thin pieces, seeds reserved
3 tbsp olive oil
2 tsp paprika
3 tbsp mayonnaise
1 tbsp wholegrain mustard
1½ tbsp honey
2 tbsp water (optional)
400 g kale, stems removed and leaves washed
125 g goats' cheese, roughly crumbled
salt and pepper to taste

Air Fryer

Preheat an air fryer to 200°C for five minutes and cook the squash for 20 minutes.

1. Preheat the oven to 210°C/190°C Fan.

2. Add the squash to a large baking sheet and coat with two tablespoons of olive oil, the paprika and salt and pepper. Roast in the oven for 25 minutes.

3. Meanwhile, rinse the seeds until all the squash is removed. Pat dry with kitchen paper and set aside.

4. Take a small mixing bowl and add the mayonnaise, mustard, half a tablespoon of honey and salt and pepper to season. Whisk to combine, loosening with the water if necessary and continuously whisking as you add it until a dressing consistency is achieved. Set aside.

5. When the squash has roasted for 25 minutes, remove from the oven and add the seeds and the remaining tablespoon of honey to the baking sheet. Shake to coat everything in honey and oil and return to the oven for a further ten minutes, reducing the oven temperature to 200°C/180°C Fan.

6. Meanwhile, add the kale leaves to a large mixing bowl and coat in the remaining tablespoon of olive oil. Season with salt and pepper and massage and scrunch with your hands for two minutes.

7. Assemble each portion of salad, layering a base of massaged kale, then the roasted squash and seeds, a tablespoon of crumbled goats' cheese and a drizzle of the creamy honey and mustard dressing. Season with lots of black pepper and enjoy!

Meal Prep Prepare all of the salad ingredients ahead of time (except the kale) and store in separate containers in the fridge. When it's time to eat, proceed from step 6.

54

Fish Finger Salad with Capers & Creamy Tartar Dressing

Low
Fat

5 min prep + 12 min cook

Calling all fish finger sandwich fans - this will be your favourite lunch! I've taken one of the best sandwiches and deconstructed it to make a creamy, tangy, crispy salad. Fish fingers are such an affordable protein source that require little to no effort on your side in terms of prep. This is my go-to lunch when I only have around 15 minutes to whip up a delicious meal. There's also the benefit of lots of the ingredients having a longer shelf life, so you can store most of the items in your fridge or freezer, and purchase the lettuce when you want to whip up the recipe in no time at all!

Serves 5

20 (2 packs) fish fingers
5 tbsp tartar sauce
1–2 tbsp water
juice of ½ lemon
2 heads of curly leaf lettuce,
    washed and torn
5 tbsp capers, drained
1 red onion, thinly sliced
salt and pepper to taste
handful of fresh dill, roughly
    chopped, to garnish

1. Preheat the grill to medium or the oven to 220°C/200°C Fan. Cook the fish fingers for 12 minutes, or until golden and crispy. Set aside to cool for a couple of minutes.

2. Add the tartar sauce to a medium-sized mixing bowl and slowly add the water and lemon juice, continuously whisking to ensure the dressing doesn't split.

3. Add the lettuce to a large bowl and drizzle over the dressing, stirring to coat the leaves.

4. Assemble each portion by layering a handful of dressed lettuce in a serving bowl. Scatter over one tablespoon of capers and a few slices of onion.

5. Top with four cooled fish fingers, a sprinkle of dill to garnish and loads of black pepper and a large pinch of salt! Time to tuck in!

Air
Fryer

To reduce energy use, cook your fish fingers in the air fryer.
Preheat to 200°C and cook for eight minutes, rotating halfway.

Salad Dressings

Cheat's Caesar

Serves 4

4 tbsp mayonnaise
½ garlic clove, crushed and smashed into a paste
  with salt
½ tbsp Dijon or wholegrain mustard
juice of ½ lemon
2 tbsp rapeseed oil
anchovies smashed into paste and grated
  Parmesan to taste (optional)
salt and pepper to taste

Whisk the mayonnaise, garlic paste, mustard
and lemon juice until combined.

Slowly stream the rapeseed oil into the mix
while vigorously whisking, or loosen with one to
two tablespoons of oil at a time while vigorously
whisking to prevent the dressing splitting.

Stir in the anchovies and Parmesan (if using),
then season generously with some salt and lots
of pepper.

Creamy Peanut

Serves 4

3 tbsp smooth peanut butter
2 tbsp soy sauce
½ garlic clove, crushed and smashed into a paste
  with salt, or ¼ tbsp garlic powder (optional)
1 tbsp rice vinegar
2 tbsp olive oil
6 tbsp water
salt to taste

Whisk the peanut butter, soy sauce, garlic
paste or powder, rice vinegar and olive oil
until combined.

Slowly add the water to the bowl and whisk
continuously to form the creamy peanut
dressing. If it is too thick, add a little more water.

Season with salt to taste.

Honey & Mustard

Serves 4

1 heaped tbsp Dijon or wholegrain mustard
1 tbsp honey
½ tbsp white wine or rice vinegar
6 tbsp extra virgin olive oil
salt and pepper to taste

Whisk the mustard, honey and vinegar in
a bowl until combined. Then slowly stream
the oil into the mix while vigorously whisking.
Season with salt and pepper to taste.

Sweet & Spicy Soy

Serves 4

2 tbsp soy sauce
1 tbsp honey
1 tsp chilli flakes, red pepper flakes or
  1 tsp sriracha
6 tbsp extra virgin olive oil
1 tbsp rice vinegar
½ garlic clove, crushed and smashed into a paste
  with salt (optional)
salt and pepper to taste

Add all the ingredients to a Mason jar and
shake to combine!

Chicken Tzatziki Bowl

15 min prep + 10 min cook

This recipe is inspired by a Greek chicken gyros, which is yoghurt-marinated chicken, loaded with various delicious ingredients, wrapped in a pitta or flatbread. To make this a salad, I've deconstructed the gyros and created a refreshing bowl packed full of protein and so much flavour. You can use it as a meal prep recipe or enjoy with friends and family. It's versatile enough to be eaten as a light lunch, but is substantial enough for a filling dinner!

Serves 5

500 g boneless, skinless chicken thighs
500 g Greek yoghurt
1 tbsp + 1 tsp dried oregano
juice of 1 lemon
6 tomatoes, roughly sliced into large chunks
1 whole cucumber, ⅓ grated, ⅔ sliced into chunks
1 red onion, thinly sliced
1 tbsp extra virgin olive oil
5 homemade flatbreads (see page 74 for Two-ingredient Flatbreads)
1 garlic clove, crushed (optional)
1 tbsp rapeseed oil
1 iceberg lettuce, washed and roughly chopped
salt and pepper to taste
large handful of fresh mint, leaves removed from tough stems, to garnish

1. Add the chicken thighs to a large mixing bowl with two tablespoons of the yoghurt, one tablespoon of oregano, the juice of half a lemon and a pinch of salt and pepper. Stir to combine and marinate in the fridge for a minimum of one hour (or up to 24 hours).

2. When it's time to eat, remove the chicken from the fridge and allow to come up to room temperature while you prepare the salad ingredients.

3. In a large bowl, add the tomatoes, chunks of cucumber, red onion, extra virgin olive oil, one teaspoon of oregano and salt and pepper to taste. Mix well and set aside. Meanwhile, make your flatbreads, or toast them if you've bought them ready-made.

4. For the tzatziki, add the remaining yoghurt, juice of half a lemon, grated cucumber and salt and pepper to a small bowl and combine. Add the garlic for more flavour, if you like.

5. Once the chicken is up to room temperature, set a large, non-stick frying pan over a high heat until piping hot. Add the rapeseed oil, then carefully add the marinated chicken thighs to the pan, frying on each side for three minutes until cooked through. Set aside on a warm plate.

6. Assemble each bowl by adding a layer of lettuce, then a serving of the tomato, cucumber and onion salad, juicy chicken thighs and a toasted flatbread. Spoon over some tzatziki and garnish with the mint leaves. Dive in!

Preheat an air fryer to 190°C and add the marinated chicken thighs (in batches if they overlap. Cook for ten minutes, then rotate and cook for a further eight minutes.

Meal Prep

The tzatziki can be made ahead of time and stored in a sealed container in the fridge for a few days. Simply stir before serving if it has separated. Store the washed and dried salad ingredients in a meal prep container lined with kitchen paper, spaced apart to prevent them from going soggy. Toast your flatbreads just before eating and enjoy the cooked chicken at room temperature. Prep the salad just before serving.

Halloumi Nourish Bowl

Veggie

5 min prep + 40 min cook

This feels like a fancy bowl that you'd order at a brunch spot. It has an array of colourful, delicious ingredients that come together beautifully as a balanced lunch or dinner, revolving of course around the star ingredient – halloumi cheese. This works perfectly as a meal prep dish and can be served hot or cold while on-the-go.

Serves 5

4 tbsp olive oil

2 tsp ground cumin

2 tsp paprika

1 large cauliflower, separated into florets, leaves roughly chopped

300 g giant couscous

1 vegetable stock cube (optional)

225 g halloumi cheese, thinly sliced

1 cucumber, finely diced

50 g spring onions, thinly sliced

large handful of fresh parsley, finely chopped, plus extra for garnish

250 g cherry tomatoes, finely chopped

juice of ½ lime, plus wedges to serve

70 g rocket

salt and pepper to taste

Preheat an air fryer to 200°C. Add the seasoned florets for seven minutes. Remove, shake or rotate the florets and add the cauliflower leaves for a further ten minutes, reducing the temperature to 180°C.

1. Preheat the oven to 210°C/190°C Fan.

2. Take a small bowl and add two tablespoons of olive oil, the ground cumin, paprika and a generous pinch of salt and pepper. Stir to combine.

3. Add the cauliflower florets to a large baking sheet and coat with half the spiced oil. Cook in the oven for 20 minutes.

4. On a separate baking sheet, add the cauliflower leaves and coat them in the remaining spiced oil. Remove the baking sheet of cauliflower florets from the oven, give it a shake to ensure even cooking and return to the oven along with the baking sheet of leaves. Continue to cook both for 15–20 minutes, or until the florets are tender and the leaves are golden and crispy.

5. Meanwhile, fill a large pan with water and bring to the boil over a medium heat, add the giant couscous, cover and leave to simmer for the time given on your packet (mine was 18 minutes). For an extra boost of flavour, add the vegetable stock cube to the water and stir to dissolve.

6. Set a non-stick frying pan over a medium heat, add one tablespoon of olive oil and fry the halloumi slices for about five minutes on one side before rotating and cooking for a further three minutes until golden. Set aside.

7. Drain and rinse the cooked couscous in a sieve with cold water until cool, then transfer to a large bowl. Add the cucumber, spring onions, parsley, tomatoes and remaining tablespoon of olive oil. Season with salt, pepper and the lime juice. Stir well to combine.

8. To serve, add a portion of each of the prepped elements to each serving bowl, along with a serving of rocket. Top with an extra sprinkle of parsley, serve with a lime wedge and enjoy!

Soups, Salads & Sides

Meal Prep Store each element separately in the fridge to maximise freshness. Fry each portion of halloumi just before serving. To enjoy this dish warm, reheat the cauliflower quickly in the air fryer for two minutes, or the microwave on high for one minute.

The Best Pan-fried Crispy Tofu

Low Fat · Low Carb · Dairy Free · Veggie · High Protein

5 min prep + 10 min cook

Note: *Really try to squeeze out as much of the moisture as you can when drying the tofu. This will maximise crispiness.*

Calling all tofu-haters, please try this recipe. It's reached Number One on Google searches for 'crispy tofu' for a good reason. The crisp exterior is loaded with umami flavour and it only takes 15 minutes to make using minimal oil and few ingredients. It's all in the method with this dish, so follow each step carefully to ensure the best tofu-tasting experience possible. Serve over rice, with noodles, in a salad or with roasted soy veggies. I can't wait for you to be converted.

Serves 4

400 g firm tofu, cubed
3 tbsp soy sauce
2 tbsp cornflour
2 tbsp rapeseed oil
1 tbsp honey

1. Start by removing the excess moisture from the cubed tofu by squeezing and patting with some kitchen paper. Add the cubes to a large bowl with one tablespoon of the soy sauce. Toss to fully coat the tofu.

2. Sift the cornflour over the tofu, tossing the cubes occasionally to ensure an even coating.

3. Add the rapeseed oil to a non-stick frying pan over a high heat. Wait until the oil is hot and then add the tofu to the pan. Evenly spread the tofu across the pan so none of the cubes are touching, otherwise they'll stick together. Leave to fry for about three minutes, or until golden and crispy on one side.

4. Add the remaining soy sauce and the honey to the hot pan and rotate the pieces of tofu, until at least two sides of each cube are super crispy. Serve however you prefer!

Crispy Baked Buffalo Cauliflower

Dairy Free **Veggie**

10 min prep + 17 min cook

These buffalo bites are a vegetarian answer to chicken nuggets. The 'buffalo' element comes from the addition of hot sauce, which is thrown all over the battered cauliflower before giving it a final roast. The result is a veggie-packed, smoky, spicy and crispy bite which will have you questioning if it's a vegetable or not. Don't throw away those leaves – add them into the batter as well to join the party. Perfect as a side dish or a movie snack.

Serves 4

3 tbsp rapeseed oil, plus extra
  for greasing
150 g plain flour
1 tsp paprika
½ tsp cayenne pepper
1 tsp ground cumin
1 tsp onion powder
½ tsp salt
1 tsp garlic powder
1 tsp baking powder
220 ml unsweetened soy milk
1 large cauliflower, separated
  into florets
4 tbsp hot sauce of choice, plus
  1 tsp
2 tbsp honey
generous pinch of flaky salt
4 tbsp mayonnaise

1. Preheat the oven to 200°C/180°C Fan. Grease a baking sheet with rapeseed oil and set aside. Line two more baking sheets with foil.

2. Combine the flour, paprika, cayenne pepper, cumin, onion powder, salt, garlic powder and baking powder in a large mixing bowl. Slowly stir the soy milk into the bowl until a smooth, thick batter forms.

3. Add the cauliflower florets to the batter mix and use a spatula to ensure all the pieces are evenly coated in the batter. The cauliflower leaves can also be evenly coated in any leftover batter and placed on the separate greased baking sheet.

4. Take the two foil-lined baking sheets and drizzle about one and a half tablespoons of rapeseed oil over each sheet. Ensure the oil is spread evenly across the sheets, then add the battered florets, one by one so they are evenly spaced and not touching each other. Pop them in the oven.

5. After about 12 minutes, the batter should be golden but not yet starting to crisp. Remove the sheets from the oven and use a slotted spatula (preferably a bendy plastic one) to rotate the pieces. Drizzle with your favourite hot sauce and the honey, moving the pieces with the spatula to ensure an even coating.

6. Return the baking sheets to the oven for another five minutes, or until crispy and golden (if your oven is powerful it could be less than this so keep an eye out!). Season the florets generously with flaky salt as soon as they are out of the oven – this will allow the salt to bind better with the bites.

7. In a small bowl, mix the mayonnaise with a teaspoon or so of hot sauce to make a chilli mayo for dipping.

Grilled Sweetcorn with Tangy Mayo & Feta

Veggie

2 min prep + 11 min cook

This recipe is inspired by Elote, a type of Mexican street corn. Traditionally, it's grilled and slathered with mayonnaise, lime juice, Cotija (a crumbly Mexican cheese) and seasoned with chilli powder and/or paprika and fresh coriander. This adaptation uses feta, which is more widely available and less expensive. When feta is finely grated (sounds odd but it works, trust me), it acts as the most delicious tangy topping to the saucy sweetcorn. It's a side that works well at a summer BBQ, but is equally delicious eaten at any time of year. Pair with your fave grilled protein and a zingy salad for corn heaven!

Serves 4

4 large corn on the cobs, husks
  removed and washed
1 tbsp rapeseed oil
2 tbsp mayonnaise
juice of ½ lime
50–100 g feta cheese
1 tsp paprika
salt and pepper to taste
handful of fresh coriander, finely
  chopped, to garnish

1. Add the corn cobs to a microwavable bowl and cover with a lid. Microwave on a medium heat for three minutes.

2. Set a non-stick frying pan over a high heat, add the rapeseed oil and cook the corn cobs for eight minutes, rotating every couple of minutes to evenly cook.

3. Meanwhile, add the mayonnaise, lime juice and a pinch of salt and pepper to a small bowl and stir to combine.

4. Coat the charred corn cobs in the mayonnaise mix and set on a serving plate. Finely grate the feta over the corn cobs and sift over a sprinkle of paprika to ensure a fine and even covering. Finely grating the feta directly over the corn will prevent clumping in your hands.

5. Garnish with the coriander and some pepper. Skip the knife and fork here, get messy and tuck in!

Air Fryer

Preheat an air fryer to 200°C. Coat the corn cobs with rapeseed oil and cook for 14 minutes, rotating halfway (no need to microwave first). Then follow steps 3-5.

Spiralised Courgette Fritters with a Soured Cream & Chive Dip

Low Carb **Veggie**

5 min prep + 20 min cook

Note: *If you don't have a spiraliser, thinly slice the courgettes into long strips, measuring about half a centimetre thick. Then slice those strips in half again. They will loosen and become bendy after salting.*

Grated courgette fritters are always delicious, but have you tried spiralised courgette fritters? Not only are they gorgeous to look at, but the increased surface area of the spirals fry up to form the crispiest exterior which offers the perfect crunch. I make a thin batter here, so every bite tastes of fresh courgette rather than heavy fried batter. Dip these fresh fritters in the tangy Soured Cream & Chive Dip for the tastiest side or snack. To scale up to a satisfying lunch, pair with a rocket side salad.

Makes 15

800 g (3 medium) courgettes, spiralised
1 tsp salt, plus extra to season
50 g self-raising flour
50 g cornflour
3 eggs
60 ml rapeseed oil
lemon wedges, to serve
salt and pepper to taste

For the dip
150 ml soured cream
juice of ½ lemon
15 g fresh chives, finely chopped
salt and pepper to taste

1. Place a sieve over a large bowl and add the spiralised courgette. Sprinkle over one teaspoon of salt and use your hands to mix together to help draw out excess moisture. Leave to drain in the sieve while you prepare the batter.

2. Take a large bowl and add the flour, cornflour and eggs. Season with salt and pepper and whisk to form a thin batter.

3. Transfer the drained courgette to a clean tea towel and squeeze out as much moisture as you can, to ensure the crispiest fritters.

4. Add the courgette to the bowl of batter mix, stirring to coat. Set a frying pan over a medium/high heat and add the rapeseed oil.

5. Take a small handful of the courgette mix, dripping with the batter, and slowly and carefully place it into the hot oil, folding the spirals onto each other in the shape of a fritter. Don't worry, they will bind together once fried. Fry the fritters in batches of five so that the pan is not overcrowded, for 3–4 minutes on each side, or until crispy.

6. Meanwhile, take a bowl and combine the soured cream, lemon juice and chives with a pinch of salt and pepper.

7. When all the fritters have been fried, set aside on a wire rack and immediately season with salt. If you want to serve them hot, pop in the oven at 140°C/120°C Fan (although they're still delicious when allowed to cool).

8. Serve the crispy fitters with lemon wedges and the Soured Cream & Chive Dip on the side.

Spicy Maple-glazed Sweet Potato Fries with Feta

20 min prep + 40 min cook

Note: *Potatoes measuring around 10–12 cm in length are the best for these sweet potato fries.*

These sweet potato fries are the best way to upgrade your fries. The sweet, paprika-y maple glaze not only provides the best flavour, it also helps to get that crispy texture without deep-frying. The crumbled feta at the end brings a whole new perspective to cheesy chips and is the perfect salty match for sweet potatoes. Pair these versatile fries with a battered protein, a grain salad or enjoy as a movie snack.

Serves 4

1 kg sweet potatoes, washed and dried
1 tbsp cornflour
2 tbsp rapeseed oil
2 tbsp maple syrup
2 tsp paprika, plus (optional) extra to serve
1 tsp salt
50 g feta cheese, crumbled
juice of ½ lime, remaining wedges sliced to serve

1. Preheat the oven to 220°C/200°C Fan. Line two baking sheets with parchment paper.

2. Slice the sweet potatoes lengthways (leaving the skin on) and chop into fries, about one and a half centimetres thick. Add to a large bowl and cover with cold water, ensuring the fries are fully submerged. Leave to soak for 30 minutes for best results. If you have less time, soak for a minimum of ten minutes.

3. Drain the fries and dry with a clean tea towel. Add to a large mixing bowl with the cornflour and rapeseed oil, stirring until the fries are evenly coated.

4. Evenly distribute the fries across the two prepared baking sheets, ensuring that they are spaced well apart to maximise crispiness. Bake in the oven for 30 minutes.

5. Meanwhile, add the maple syrup, paprika and salt to a small mixing bowl and combine.

6. After 30 minutes, remove the fries from the oven, drizzle over the maple syrup and paprika mix and shake to coat the pieces evenly. Return to the oven for ten minutes or until crispy.

7. Serve with a crumble of feta, a squeeze of lime juice, a lime wedge on the side and an optional sprinkle of paprika.

Preheat an air fryer to 200°C. Cook the sweet potato fries for 25 minutes and then toss in the maple syrup and paprika glaze. Cook for a further ten minutes.

Soups, Salads & Sides

Cavolo Nero with Garlic & Lemon

Gluten Free · Low Carb · Vegan

7 min prep + 8 min cook

If a friend or family member hates cavolo nero, I whip this recipe up in 15 minutes to change their mind. We've all tried baked kale and enjoyed it – but how about taking its classier cousin and adding some tang, spice and garlic (always plenty of garlic!), to take the dish to the next level. This is one of my favourite sides and I could probably eat the whole lot if no one was around to take it off me. If you're not a fan of spice, simply leave out the chilli flakes or switch with milder red pepper flakes.

Serves 4

150 g cavolo nero
juice of ½ lemon
1 tsp chilli flakes or red pepper flakes
2–3 garlic cloves, crushed
1½ tbsp extra virgin olive oil
pinch of salt
pinch of flaky salt

1. Preheat the oven to 200°C/180°C Fan. Line a baking sheet with parchment paper and set aside.

2. Start by removing the cavolo nero leaves from the stem. I do this by creating a little tear on each side of the toughest part of the stem and then running my hand along it which removes the leaves perfectly. Tear the leaves into medium-sized rectangles (bite-sized pieces).

3. In a large bowl, combine the lemon juice, chilli flakes and garlic with the olive oil and a pinch of salt. Add the torn cavolo nero leaves to the bowl and toss, ensuring every piece is coated in the mix.

4. Place the cavolo nero onto the prepared baking sheet. Spread the pieces so they're evenly spaced and pop in the oven for 6–8 minutes.

5. Serve with a pinch of flaky salt and enjoy! Pair this recipe with battered fish/chicken, your favourite pasta dish or noodles. It's pretty versatile so it works alongside a lot of foods!

Air Fryer

Preheat an air fryer to 190°C and follow steps 1-3. Add the kale to the air fryer basket. Cook for 4-6 minutes, or until crispy.

Two-ingredient Flatbreads

20 min prep + 20 min cook

I always presumed flatbreads required a massive amount of effort – constant kneading, loads of ingredients, lots of patience and skill. However, as soon as I made them for the first time, I realised that with two simple ingredients and 25 minutes of your time, you can easily whip up your own for a fraction of the price of shop-bought. All without compromising on flavour, of course. They're such a versatile side – paired with a curry, a salad bowl, as a lunch wrap or a pizza base – the options are endless!

Makes 8 small or 6 large

250 g Greek yoghurt
250 g self-raising flour, plus extra for dusting
2 sprays of vegetable oil or rapeseed oil per flatbread

1. In a large mixing bowl, add the yoghurt and flour and combine. Turn out onto a floured surface and knead into a dough. If the dough feels too sticky, add a little more flour.

2. Set the dough to one side and allow to rest for 15–20 minutes.

3. After the dough has rested, divide it into eight smaller balls or six larger balls.

4. Sprinkle some flour over a work surface and a rolling pin and roll out each ball into a round shape (about half a centimetre thick).

5. Meanwhile, heat a non-stick frying pan over a medium heat for a few minutes, spraying two pumps of oil into the pan to stop each flatbread sticking. Place a flatbread into the pan and cook for one minute. When bubbles appear on the surface, flip the flatbread and cook for a further minute on the other side. Ensure both sides are golden brown before transferring to a warm plate.

6. Continue to cook all the flatbreads in the same way. This will take about 20 minutes, but it's well worth it!

74

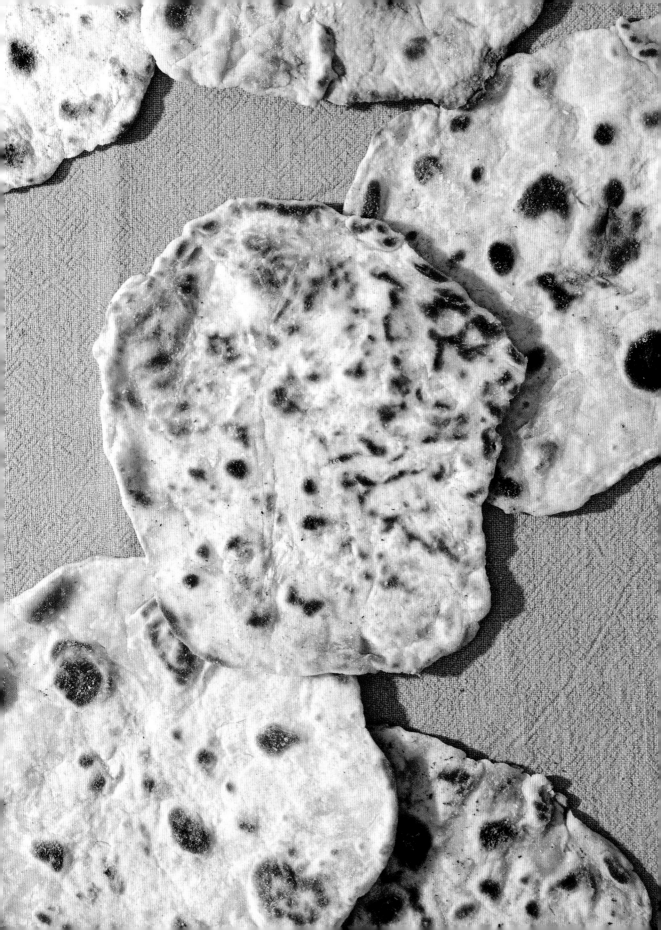

Whipped Feta Dip with Harissa

Freeze　**Veggie**

10 min prep

When making a homemade dip, I really want it to be worthwhile and stand up to a pre-made, affordable version. It needs to come together quickly, have a short ingredients list and, preferably, require no cooking. Enter my whipped creamy feta with spicy harissa. You can make this recipe in around ten minutes and it looks so stunning if you're in the mood to impress. I love pairing this dip with toasted flatbreads (see Two-ingredient Flatbreads on page 74) – they act as the perfect vehicle to scoop up the saucy whipped feta. You can use any toasted, crusty bread though or even crisps. A healthier option could be to dip cold veggies such as cucumber sticks, carrot batons or baby gem lettuce leaves.

Serves 4

200 g feta cheese
200 g low fat cream cheese
juice of ½ lemon
1 garlic clove, crushed
1 tbsp harissa paste
1 tbsp extra virgin olive oil
320 g (4-pack) flatbreads (or Two-ingredient Flatbreads, see page 74)
salt to taste
pinch of paprika, to garnish
1 tbsp chopped fresh parsley, to garnish

1. Put the feta, cream cheese, lemon juice and garlic into a food processor. Season with salt and process on high until whipped. This will take around two minutes.

2. In a small bowl, combine the harissa paste with the olive oil and season with a pinch of salt.

3. Toast the flatbreads in a toaster or a dry frying pan and set aside.

4. Transfer the feta mix into a serving bowl and drizzle over the harissa oil, swirling the oil into the dip slightly for a more pleasing look. Add a pinch of paprika and a sprinkle of fresh parsley. Dip those flatbreads to your heart's content!

Weeknight Winners

Pink Pasta

Freeze   Veggie

5 min prep + 40 min cook

This is a hybrid of two hugely popular viral recipes, which combines the baked feta trend with the pink pasta trend. You might be sceptical of what this tastes like, as pasta usually isn't hot pink. However, trust me on this one - the roasted beetroot, shallots and garlic blend with the rich and tangy feta to form the most delicious sauce. If you're willing to share, serve this to guests to wow them with the flavour and colour of this comforting pasta dish.

Serves 4

250 g beetroot, washed thoroughly and roughly chopped
6 garlic cloves, skin removed and left whole
300 g shallots, sliced in half
1 tbsp extra virgin olive oil
200 g feta cheese, plus extra to garnish
300 g rigatoni
juice of ½ lemon
salt and pepper to taste
large handful of roughly chopped fresh mint or basil, to garnish
pinch of chilli flakes (optional)

1. Preheat the oven to 200°C/180°C Fan.

2. Add the beetroot, garlic and shallots to a baking sheet. Coat with the olive oil and a generous pinch of salt. Cover the baking sheet with foil and pop in the oven for 15 minutes.

3. Remove from the oven, peel back the foil and add the block of feta to the beetroot mix, carefully rotating to coat in the oil that is already on the baking sheet. Replace the foil and return to the oven for a further 15–20 minutes.

4. Meanwhile, fill a large pan with salted water and bring to the boil. Add the rigatoni to the pan and set the timer for the packet time given, minus one minute so that the pasta is al dente. Drain the cooked pasta, reserving a generous amount of pasta water. Return the pasta to the pan.

5. Add the contents of the baking sheet to a blender with two ladles of the reserved pasta water and the lemon juice. Blend until smooth, then pour into the pan containing the drained pasta. Continue to cook over a low heat until the sauce thickens to the desired consistency. Serve with a side of greens, a sprinkle of fresh mint or basil and a pinch of chilli flakes if you like some heat. If you have any spare feta, feel free to add an extra crumble on top!

Mushroom Rigatoni Ragù

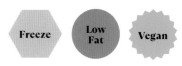

Freeze • Low Fat • Vegan

5 min prep + 25 min cook

I challenge you to serve this to a meat eater and ask them if they feel like it's missing something. The answer (I hope) will be that it ticks all the boxes for their pasta needs. The finely chopped mushrooms make the best base for a meatless ragù, which, by the way, only requires 7–8 ingredients. Once you get past the chopping of the mushrooms, it's smooth sailing with very little attention needed as you fry. The toasted basil breadcrumbs serve as the best finisher to this dish, offering a crunch against the saucy ragù. You'll question whether you ever need to use cheese again!

Serves 4

3 tbsp extra virgin olive oil
250 g chestnut mushrooms, finely chopped
1 red onion, finely chopped
8 tbsp tomato purée
3 garlic cloves, crushed
400 g rigatoni
35 g panko breadcrumbs
3 tbsp finely chopped fresh basil
pinch of flaky salt
salt and pepper to taste

1. Put two tablespoons of the olive oil into a deep frying pan over a medium heat. Add the mushrooms, season with salt and pepper and cook for five minutes, stirring frequently.

2. Add the onion to the pan and cook for a further 5–8 minutes, reducing the heat to medium/low. All the excess moisture needs to evaporate so that the mushrooms and onion can start to take on some colour and caramelise.

3. Next, add the tomato purée and garlic to gently fry in the mushroom and onion mix. At the same time, fill a pan with salted water, bring to the boil and add the rigatoni. Set the timer to the packet time given, minus two minutes so that the cooked pasta is al dente. Continue to stir and gently fry the tomato and mushroom mix while the pasta cooks.

4. Reserve three ladles of the pasta water before draining the cooked rigatoni and transferring it to the deep frying pan. Add all three ladles of pasta water to the pan and stir over a low heat to coat the rigatoni in the sauce. Continue to cook until the pasta water has emulsified to form a glossy, delicious tomato sauce.

5. Meanwhile, take a separate frying pan and add the remaining tablespoon of olive oil, the panko breadcrumbs, basil (reserving some to garnish) and flaky salt. Gently fry for two minutes until the breadcrumb mix has turned golden.

6. Serve the mushroom ragù with a sprinkling of the crunchy toasted basil breadcrumbs and an additional garnish of basil. So damn good.

Rigatoni alla Carbonara

5 min prep + 18 min cook

This recipe is very close to my heart, as carbonara is not only my favourite pasta dish, it's also my favourite meal, full stop. I've always been hesitant to release a carbonara recipe as I've wanted to do it justice, but after many, many rounds of testing, I think I've hopefully done that with this version. Traditionally in Italy, carbonara is served with spaghetti, however, I love to use rigatoni. The tubes are the perfect shape to collect the ideal ratio of deliciously flavourful sauce to pasta with every bite. Plus, a surprise morsel of pancetta nestled within the rigatoni is always welcome! Whip this up for friends or family as a low-maintenance, high-satisfaction crowd-pleaser.

Serves 4

1 tbsp olive oil
160 g pancetta, cubed
400 g rigatoni
5 egg yolks, plus 1 whole egg
60 g Parmesan, finely grated, plus extra to serve
2 tsp pepper, plus extra to taste
salt to taste

1. Set a large frying pan over a low heat and add the olive oil and pancetta to gently fry for about eight minutes until the fat has rendered nicely but the cubes are not yet crispy.

2. Fill a large pan with salted water and bring to the boil, then add the rigatoni and cook for about five minutes. As the pasta cooks, take a bowl and add the egg yolks, whole egg, Parmesan, two teaspoons of pepper and a pinch of salt and whisk to combine. Continue to gently fry the pancetta while the pasta is cooking.

3. Just after the five minutes of cooking time, transfer four tablespoons of the pasta water to the bowl containing the Parmesan and egg mix and stir to combine. This will temper the eggs, bringing them up to an appropriate temperature.

4. Once the rigatoni has cooked until just under the amount of time given on your packet, reserve a mugful of pasta water before draining and transferring the pasta to the pan with the pancetta. Use tongs to toss and coat the rigatoni in the pancetta fat.

5. Remove from the heat and allow the pan to cool for a couple of minutes, then add the tempered Parmesan and egg mix and stir to combine. Loosen with the reserved pasta water if necessary, as the Parmesan will absorb a lot of water.

6. Serve immediately with more pepper and salt if necessary and a sprinkling of extra Parmesan.

Pork Stroganoff Orzo

Freeze

5 min prep + 20 min cook

Take a delicious, creamy sauce and combine it with one of the most versatile and popular pasta shapes around, and you produce a dish that can be enjoyed all year round. Serve it up as a hearty winter warmer or enjoy the freshness of the crème fraîche and lemon in the sunshine. Pork loins are an affordable cut of meat and when seared quickly over a high heat the flavour that the meat imparts to the stroganoff is just 'chef's kiss'. I've made a few stroganoff recipes and I have to say that this one takes home the gold.

Serves 4

1½ tbsp rapeseed oil
4 pork loins, about 480 g total weight
1 onion, finely diced
250 g mushrooms, thinly sliced
3–4 garlic cloves, finely chopped
320 g orzo
120 ml crème fraîche
600 ml chicken stock
1½ tbsp cornflour
2 tbsp boiling water
1 tbsp Dijon mustard
1 tbsp soy sauce or Worcestershire sauce
juice of ½ lemon
salt and pepper to taste
large handful of chopped fresh parsley, to garnish (optional)

1. Add one tablespoon of the rapeseed oil to a large, deep pan and set over a high heat. Fry the pork loins for three minutes on each side until nicely browned. Remove and slice the pork into bite-sized pieces, removing any excess fat. Set aside.

2. Deglaze the sticky meaty bits in the pan with a splash of hot water. Add the remaining rapeseed oil to the pan with the onion. Reduce the heat to medium/low and fry the onion with some salt and pepper for about four minutes until softened.

3. Add the mushrooms to the pan, lightly frying until the moisture is released and cooked off and the mushrooms have softened. Add the garlic for the final minute of frying.

4. Bring a separate deep pan of salted water to the boil and add the orzo. Set your timer for two minutes less than the packet cook time.

5. Meanwhile, put the crème fraîche in a bowl, add a splash of the chicken stock, stirring to heat/temper the crème fraîche to prevent it from splitting. Pour the rest of the chicken stock into the pan containing the mushrooms and onion. Add the reserved pork pieces. Pour the crème fraîche into the pan and stir to combine.

6. Make a cornflour slurry by mixing the cornflour with the water in a bowl. Add the mustard, soy sauce, lemon juice and a pinch of salt and lots of pepper, then add the cornflour slurry to the pan, stirring until the sauce starts to thicken. By this time the orzo should be al dente. Drain the pasta and add to the pan, stirring to combine and loosening with a splash of pasta water if necessary. Garnish with fresh parsley, if you like, and dig in!

Harissa Yoghurt Orzo

 Freeze Low Fat Veggie

5 min prep + 15 min cook

Harissa is a red pepper paste infused with rose petals that is used in North African and Middle Eastern cuisines. In many harissa dishes, cool yoghurt is used to offset the spice and this natural winning combo inspired me to balance out a tomatoey harissa-infused pasta sauce with a generous helping of yoghurt swirled through. The result is a creamy, tangy, mild sauce with a hint of spice that is so, so good. Courgette is the perfect addition to bump up the nutrients in the sauce and orzo acts as the ideal vehicle for forking up big, comforting mouthfuls. It's great for meal prep or sharing with friends and family, taking 20 minutes to prep and cook (with time to spare for clean up!).

Serves 5

2 courgettes, grated
1 tbsp extra virgin olive oil
1 onion, diced
500 g orzo
4 garlic cloves, crushed
grated zest and juice of ½ lemon
70 g sun-dried tomatoes, thinly
  sliced
4 tbsp harissa
4 tbsp tomato purée
4–5 tbsp Greek yoghurt
salt and pepper to taste
handful of fresh parsley, roughly
  chopped, to garnish

Meal Prep

Divide individual servings
into meal prep containers
once cooked and chill for up
to three days in the fridge,
or store in the freezer for
up to three months. Defrost
in the fridge overnight. When
it's time to reheat, add one
tablespoon of water to the meal
prep container and heat in
the microwave on high for two
minutes. Serve with an extra
dollop of fresh yoghurt and a
sprinkle of chopped parsley.

1. Pile the grated courgette into a clean tea towel and generously season with salt. Squeeze thoroughly to remove the excess moisture and set aside.

2. Set a large, deep, non-stick frying pan over a medium heat, add the olive oil, onion and salt and pepper to taste and fry for four minutes.

3. Meanwhile, bring a large pan of salted water to the boil and add the orzo. Cook for two minutes less than the packet cooking time.

4. Add the garlic, lemon zest, sun-dried tomatoes, three tablespoons of the harissa, the grated courgette and tomato purée to the frying pan. Fry over a medium heat until the moisture from the courgette cooks off and the tomato purée darkens in colour. Continue to fry as the orzo cooks. If you think the tomato purée is starting to burn, add a splash of pasta water.

5. Drain, then transfer the orzo directly to the frying pan with 300 millilitres of the pasta water and the lemon juice. Continue to cook for two minutes, stirring frequently.

6. Once the sauce has thickened and the orzo is cooked, add four tablespoons of the yoghurt to the pan and stir to combine. Swirl in the rest of the harissa and garnish with the parsley. Season with an extra grind of salt and pepper and serve with an optional extra dollop of yoghurt.

Spicy Spaghetti with Mussels & Crispy Breadcrumbs

Dairy Free

5 min prep + 17 min cook

This recipe tastes like summer in a bowl. The flavours are inspired by both spaghetti aglio e olio (parsley, garlic, lemon and extra virgin olive oil) and spaghetti *alle vongole* - traditionally made with clams, although I've used mussels. The hybrid of flavours results in the most refreshing pasta dish. You may think that this recipe isn't within budget, but purchasing de-shelled, frozen cooked mussels is cheaper than chicken! I was so pleasantly surprised when I found them in the freezer section of my supermarket. Don't skip on the crispy breadcrumb topping – it's the perfect crunchy contrast to the silky pasta and soft mussels. Enjoy with friends or family in the garden, or inside in the winter when you want to pretend it's summer.

Serves 5

6 tbsp extra virgin olive oil
70 g panko breadcrumbs
5 garlic cloves, thinly sliced
½–1 tbsp chilli flakes, plus extra to garnish
30 g fresh parsley, stems and leaves separated and both finely chopped
500 g spaghetti
grated zest and juice of ½–1 lemon
400 g frozen cooked mussels, defrosted in the fridge
salt and pepper to taste

1. Set a large, non-stick frying pan over a medium heat, add one tablespoon of the olive oil and the panko breadcrumbs. Season with salt and pepper and fry for five minutes until toasted and golden. Transfer the breadcrumbs to a plate and set aside.

2. Add the remaining five tablespoons of olive oil to the same frying pan along with the garlic, chilli flakes (to your taste) and parsley stems. Season with salt and pepper and gently fry over a low heat to prevent the garlic from burning.

3. Meanwhile, set a large pan filled with heavily salted water over a medium heat and bring to the boil. Add the spaghetti and cook for two minutes less than the packet cooking time.

4. Once the pasta has cooked, the garlic should be golden and almost caramelised. Drain the pasta, adding 300 millilitres of the pasta water and the undercooked spaghetti to the frying pan. Squeeze over most of the lemon juice and add the mussels.

5. Continue to warm over a low heat, stirring gently until the pasta water has created a glossy sauce that coats the spaghetti. Sprinkle over most of the chopped parsley leaves and the lemon zest and stir until combined.

6. Serve each portion with a garnish of crispy toasted breadcrumbs, a pinch of chilli flakes to taste, the remaining parsley leaves and a final squeeze of lemon juice.

Creamy Tuna Pasta Bake

5 min prep + 25 min cook

If you're a fan of a tuna/mayo/sweetcorn combo, this should be your go-to pasta bake. It's the recipe that my friends send me excited texts about and I think that's for a few reasons. Firstly, somehow it comes together in 30 minutes, making it quick and easy for a weeknight. Secondly, I take a shortcut that I believe adds more flavour than rival tuna pasta bake recipes – the cream cheese eliminates the need for a roux, which reduces the ingredients list and saves time. Plus, it tastes so, so good and I've been guilty of consuming the entire dish over a two-day period on my own, so I hope you enjoy it as much as I do.

Serves 6

400 g rigatoni
1 tbsp olive oil
1 onion, finely diced
2 garlic cloves, finely chopped
3 x 145 g cans tuna (in brine),
　drained
200 g cream cheese
100 g Cheddar, grated
juice of ¼ lemon
2 tsp Dijon mustard
1 x 260 g can sweetcorn kernels,
　drained
salt and pepper to taste
large handful of fresh parsley,
　roughly torn, to garnish

1. Preheat the grill to medium.

2. Fill a large pan with salted water and bring to the boil. Add the rigatoni to the pan and set the timer to the packet time given, minus two minutes, so that the pasta is al dente. Drain the pasta, reserving three ladles of the pasta water for later.

3. Next, put the olive oil in another pan over a low/medium heat and add the onion. Gently fry for around five minutes until softened (not caramelised). Add the garlic and fry for another two minutes.

4. Add the tuna, cream cheese, 60 grams of the Cheddar and two ladles of the pasta water you reserved earlier. Stir until the cheese melts and a creamy sauce has formed. Add the extra ladle of pasta water as necessary if the sauce needs to be loosened further.

5. Stir the lemon juice and mustard into the sauce and season with salt and lots of pepper. Pour the rigatoni, sweetcorn and creamy tuna sauce into an ovenproof dish (about 30 cm x 25 cm). Stir to incorporate everything and sprinkle over the remaining 40 grams of Cheddar. Pop under the grill for ten minutes, or until the cheese is golden and crispy.

6. Top with fresh parsley to serve.

Spinach & Ricotta Pasta Bake

Veggie

5 min prep + 30 min cook

This recipe was inspired by spinach and ricotta stuffed pasta shells. If you haven't seen or tried them, the pasta shells are usually large and you have to spend time individually stuffing each one with a filling. This version lowers the cost and effort significantly. Standard conchiglie is cheaper, but just as delicious and the creamy ricotta, spinach and pasta mix mimics the 'stuffed' aspect without the hassle. It's assembled with just three simple layers - spinach and ricotta shells, tomato sauce and mozzarella - which all combine to create the most comforting dinner that's perfect for a crowd.

Serves 6

500 g frozen spinach
2 x 400 g cans plum tomatoes
1 onion, diced
2 tsp dried oregano
3 garlic cloves, crushed
1 tbsp olive oil
400 ml vegetable stock
500 g conchiglie
2 x 250 g packs ricotta
1 egg
200 g mozzarella, grated
salt and pepper to taste
small handful of fresh basil,
  to garnish

1. Preheat the oven to 220°C/200°C Fan.

2. Take a heatproof jug or bowl, add the spinach and cover with boiling water to defrost.

3. In a food processor, add the plum tomatoes, onion, oregano, garlic and salt and pepper and blitz together until smooth.

4. Set a pan over a medium heat, add the olive oil, the blended tomato mix and the stock and cook for ten minutes.

5. Meanwhile, set a large pan of salted water over a medium heat, bring to the boil and add the pasta. Simmer for two minutes less than the amount of cooking time given on your packet.

6. While the pasta is cooking, take a deep ovenproof dish, add the ricotta and egg and season with salt and pepper before mixing together. Drain and squeeze the defrosted spinach to get rid of any excess liquid. Add this to the ricotta mix and stir until combined.

7. Drain the pasta, reserving half a mugful of pasta water and add both to the dish, stirring to combine with the spinach and ricotta mix. Pour over the blended tomato sauce and then add a layer of grated mozzarella.

8. Pop in the oven for 15–20 minutes, or until the cheese has melted and turned golden. Top with fresh basil leaves to garnish and serve yourself a large helping!

Pizza Bowls

 Freeze   Low Carb   High Protein

5 min prep + 25 min cook

Note: *Make your own Italian seasoning: 1 tsp dried basil, 1 tsp dried oregano and 1 tsp dried thyme or rosemary.*

A low-carb, high-protein dream, the oven does all the hard work for you here. The vegetable and sausage mix takes on some colour and flavour in the first stage of roasting, before the pizza-inspired sauce and toppings are added. It's such a delicious way to incorporate more vegetables into your day - feel free to switch up the veg according to your preferences.

Serves 5

2 courgettes, chopped and cubed
1 aubergine, chopped and cubed
200 g mushrooms, thinly sliced
8 pork sausages (454 g), casing removed and roughly torn
2 tbsp olive oil
1 tbsp Italian seasoning
pinch of chilli flakes (optional)
1 x 500 g carton passata
250 g mozzarella, grated
salt and pepper to taste
fresh jalapeño, thinly sliced, to garnish (optional)
3 tbsp finely chopped fresh chives, to garnish

1. Preheat the oven to 220°C/200°C Fan.

2. To a large bowl, add the veggies and torn sausage pieces. Add the olive oil, Italian seasoning and salt and pepper to taste. If you like spice, add a pinch of chilli flakes. Toss to incorporate all the ingredients.

3. Take five 15-centimetre ramekins and divide the veggie and sausage mix equally between them. Pop in the oven for 15 minutes to brown or take on some colour.

4. Remove carefully from the oven, add a serving of passata to each ramekin and stir to combine. Top each with a layer of mozzarella and return to the oven for a further ten minutes, or until the cheese is golden and melted.

5. Top each ramekin with slices of jalapeño (if using) and a sprinkling of fresh chives to garnish.

 Meal Prep   Follow steps 2-3 and store the individual ramekins in the fridge for up to three days. When it's time to eat, follow steps 4-5 - the cheese is better melted fresh.

The Best Burrito Bowl

5 min prep + 25 min cook

I never get bored of this recipe as there are so many different components within one bowl that offer a variety of textures, nutrients and flavours. Use it for meal prep or serve to friends and family as a buffet-style dinner party where your guests can pick and mix. If you don't have an air fryer for the chicken, preheat your oven to 220°C/200°C Fan. Cook the chicken for 15 minutes, then rotate and cook for a further ten minutes. Following the method below, everything comes together in under half an hour, so there's no excuse not to make your own burrito bowls – they are the ultimate healthy comfort food!

Serves 6

400 g white rice, thoroughly rinsed
320 g (1 can) sweetcorn kernels, microwaved for 2 minutes
1 iceberg lettuce, chopped

For the chicken
600 g boneless, skinless chicken thighs
1 tbsp rapeseed oil
1 tsp chilli powder
1 tsp smoked paprika
1 tsp ground cumin
1 tsp dried oregano
salt and pepper to taste

For the refried beans
400 ml gluten-free beef stock
2 x 400 g cans black beans, drained and rinsed
½ tsp ground cumin

For the salsa
500 g or 6 large salad tomatoes, finely diced
bunch of fresh coriander, roughly chopped, plus extra to garnish
½ red onion, finely diced
juice of ½ lime, plus wedges to serve
1 tbsp extra virgin olive oil

1. For the chicken, add the chicken thighs, rapeseed oil, spices and oregano to a large bowl. Mix together to ensure the meat is evenly coated, then place the thighs in the air fryer to cook at 190°C for ten minutes. Rotate and cook for a further ten minutes.

2. Once the chicken is golden and cooked through, remove from the air fryer and set aside on a wire rack. Season with salt.

3. Meanwhile, cook your rice in a large pan of boiling water according to the packet instructions. Mine cooked in 12 minutes. Drain.

4. For the refried beans, to a heatproof measuring jug, add the beef stock, black beans and ground cumin. Using a stick blender, blitz a few times to a nice chunky consistency. Add the beans to a deep pan and set over a medium heat for about six minutes until reduced and thickened. As the beans cool, the mixture will thicken even more. Set aside.

5. For the salsa, put the tomatoes in a sieve, season generously with salt and toss around to remove excess moisture without having to go through the pain of deseeding!

6. Add the tomatoes, half the coriander, the red onion, half the lime juice and the extra virgin olive oil to a bowl. Season with salt and pepper and stir to combine.

7. Add the remaining coriander to the cooked rice with the rest of the lime juice and season with salt and pepper, if you like. You could have the rice plain, if you prefer.

8. Chop the spicy chicken into bite-sized pieces. Serve up with a portion of rice, some refried beans, sweetcorn and lettuce. Top with a generous spoonful or two of the salsa. Serve with a lime wedge and an extra sprinkle of coriander.

Meal Prep

```
Store each prepared component of the burrito bowl in a separate sealed container to
maximise freshness and chill in the fridge for up to three days. When it's time to
eat, add a serving of the ingredients: rice, chicken, refried beans and sweetcorn
to a bowl and microwave on high for two minutes. Then add a serving of lettuce and
salsa to your bowl and dig in.
```

Halloumi Curry

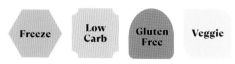

Freeze *Low Carb* *Gluten Free* *Veggie*

5 min prep + 25 min cook

For a few years, this was the most popular recipe on my website, so when deciding what 'classics' to include in my book, this went straight to the top of the list. I think people loved the combination of such a popular ingredient (hello, halloumi) with a creamy yet rich curry sauce. You can opt for kale as a cheaper alternative to cavolo nero. I love a vegetarian-inclusive recipe and I love it even more when it's made in around 30 minutes. If you're curious about the fusion of a salty cheese with curry flavours, try this out for your next dinner and prepare to have your mind blown.

Serves 5

1 tbsp rapeseed oil
450 g (2 packs) low-fat halloumi cheese, sliced into thin chunks
1 onion, finely diced
4 garlic cloves, crushed
1 tbsp curry powder
1 tbsp garam masala
1 tsp ground turmeric
1 tbsp peeled and finely grated fresh ginger
2 x 500 g cartons passata
400 ml gluten-free vegetable stock
150 g bag cavolo nero, stems removed and torn into small pieces
150 ml single cream
juice of ½ lime, remaining wedges to serve
350 g white rice, rinsed and cooked according to packet instructions
salt to taste
1 tbsp roughly chopped fresh mint, to garnish
red pepper flakes or chilli flakes (optional)

1. Set a large, deep, non-stick pan over a medium heat, add half a tablespoon of the rapeseed oil and fry the halloumi until golden and crispy, for about two minutes on each side. Set the halloumi aside.

2. Add the remaining rapeseed oil to the pan. Add the onion and gently fry, seasoning with a pinch of salt, for around four minutes, or until softened.

3. Next, put the garlic, ground spices and ginger into the pan and fry for two minutes until the spices smell fragrant.

4. Pour the passata into the pan and then the stock. Cook for ten minutes, uncovered, over a medium/low heat.

5. Add the cavolo nero pieces and half of the fried halloumi to the pan. Stir to combine and pop the lid on. Cook for a further five minutes.

6. Reduce the heat and stir the cream and lime juice into the pan. Add salt to taste. Serve with a portion of rice, some crispy reserved halloumi and fresh mint on top, plus a lime wedge. If you love a bit of heat, add a pinch of red pepper flakes or chilli flakes before devouring.

Slow Cooker

```
Add the ingredients used in steps 2-4 to your slow
cooker and cook on low for four hours. When it's
time to eat, cook the rice and follow step 1, then
steps 5-6 to serve.
```

Peanut Chicken Curry with Crispy Baked Kale

5 min prep + 20 min cook

I had to include this recipe in my book as of all the lovely photos that I receive from you guys, this curry probably features the most. It's creamy and rich in flavour thanks to the peanut butter and coconut milk and it comes together in under 30 minutes so is ideal for a weeknight dinner. It's great for meal prep, too, as it's freezable and you're guaranteed to never get bored of it. I'd go as far as to say it's possibly my favourite curry recipe, so if you're a peanut butter fan I strongly urge you to start with this dish.

Serves 5

250 g brown rice, thoroughly rinsed
50 g spring onions, rinsed
2 tbsp olive oil
600 g boneless, skinless chicken breasts, thinly sliced into pieces
1½ tbsp curry powder
3 garlic cloves, crushed
4 tbsp crunchy peanut butter
1½ tbsp soy sauce
pinch of flaky salt
juice of ½ lime, plus remaining cut into wedges to serve
1 x 400 g can coconut milk
400 ml vegetable stock
200 g kale
salt to taste
pinch of chilli flakes (optional)

Add the ingredients used in steps 3-6 to your slow cooker. Cook on high for two hours or low for three to four hours.

1. Preheat the oven to 200°C/180°C Fan.

2. Add the rice to a medium pan with a 2:1 ratio of water to rice. Set the timer according to the packet time given (mine was 18 minutes) and simmer until cooked. Drain and set aside.

3. Meanwhile, chop the spring onions in half, dividing the greener half and the lighter half of the onion. Slice the greener half on a bias (diagonally), setting aside to use as a garnish, and chop the white half more roughly to add to the sauce.

4. To a large pan, add one tablespoon of the olive oil, the sliced white spring onions and the chicken pieces and gently fry over a medium heat for about four minutes. Add the curry powder and garlic to fry for a further minute.

5. Add the peanut butter, soy sauce, flaky salt and lime juice to the pan over a low heat. This will be a very thick mix, so add a splash of coconut milk to help loosen it up.

6. Slowly pour in the rest of the coconut milk, stirring continuously. When fully combined, add the vegetable stock. Reduce to a low simmer and set the timer to 15 minutes.

7. In the meantime, wash the kale and put on a large baking sheet with the remaining olive oil. Season generously with salt. Use your hands to make sure all the kale bits get an even coating of oil. Pop in the oven for 7–10 minutes to get nice and crispy.

8. Serve the chicken curry with a portion of cooked rice, the crispy baked kale and a lime wedge. Garnish with the reserved spring onions and a pinch of chilli flakes if you like it hot.

Saag Paneer with Rice & Naan

5 min prep + 15 min cook

This is a nutrient-dense, warming, comforting meal that can be whipped up in just 20 minutes! It's a simplified version of one of the most popular Indian takeaway items on the menu. I use frozen spinach as it's cost effective for the large amount of spinach that needs to be used in this recipe. It's the perfect dish to make for friends or family when you want to impress with minimal stress or effort on your part.

Serves 4

2 tbsp rapeseed oil
225 g (1 block) paneer, cut into 2 cm cubes
200 g white rice
1 onion, diced
4 garlic cloves, crushed
1½ tbsp peeled and grated fresh ginger
2 tsp garam masala
500 g frozen spinach
400 ml vegetable stock
4 mini naans
1 lemon, cut into ¼ wedges, to serve
4 tbsp natural yoghurt, to serve (optional)
salt and pepper to taste

1. Set a deep, non-stick pan over a medium heat, add one tablespoon of the rapeseed oil and fry the paneer cubes, rotating them every two minutes until each side is lightly golden. Set aside on a plate and season generously with salt.

2. Meanwhile, set a large pan of water over a medium heat and add the rice to cook for the amount of time given on the packet.

3. Add the remaining rapeseed oil and the onion to the pan that the paneer was cooked in. Season with salt and fry over a low heat for five minutes until the onion turns translucent. Add the garlic, ginger and garam masala, allowing the spices and aromatics to fry for a minute until fragrant.

4. Add the frozen spinach and vegetable stock, increase the heat to medium, bring to a simmer and cover with a lid. Continue to cook until the rice is ready.

5. Add half of the spinach mix to a blender and blitz until smooth. Add back to the pan and stir to combine. Meanwhile, put the mini naans on to toast.

6. To serve, add a portion of rice and spinach to each bowl. Top with a few cubes of the crispy paneer and serve with a wedge of lemon and a mini naan. Encourage your friends to squeeze the lemon wedge over the whole bowl and use the naan to scoop up big flavourful mouthfuls! An optional tablespoon of natural yoghurt on the side is a nice addition.

Meal Prep

Divide individual portions into sealed containers, adding a serving of rice and a few ladles of spinach and paneer to each. Chill in the fridge for up to three days. When it's time to eat, heat in the microwave on high for two minutes while you toast your naan.

Spicy Butter & Tomato White Fish with Vegetables

5 min prep + 40 min cook

This is one of the tastiest fish recipes I have ever developed. It's mildly spicy (you can turn up the heat if you want to), rich, buttery and so fresh at the same time. Whatever mood I'm in, this dish immediately comforts and de-stresses me. I use frozen fish here as it's cheaper than fresh fish and great to have in the freezer so that you can whip this up whenever you want. Serve it with rice, greens or a side salad, depending on your mood. For me it's a firm favourite for weekly meal prep, but if you're willing to share, it's a great low-stress dinner party meal.

Serves 5

2 courgettes, sliced into diagonal semi-circles
1 red onion, cut into thin wedges
2 tbsp extra virgin olive oil
2 garlic cloves, crushed
3 tsp chilli flakes
50 g butter
520 g frozen white fish fillets, defrosted
handful of fresh basil, stems finely chopped
2 x 400 g cans cherry tomatoes
salt and pepper to taste

1. Preheat the oven to 220°C/200°C Fan.

2. Add the courgettes and red onion to an ovenproof pan and add the olive oil and a pinch of salt and pepper. Mix to fully coat the vegetables and place the pan in the oven for 20 minutes.

3. Meanwhile, prepare the spicy butter by adding the garlic, two teaspoons of the chilli flakes and the butter to a heatproof bowl, before heating in the microwave on high for around 30 seconds until melted. Season with salt and pepper.

4. Pat the defrosted fish with kitchen paper to dry it and place in a large bowl. Drizzle the spicy butter over the pieces and gently mix to coat the fish, ensuring you don't break the fish up.

5. Remove the vegetables from the oven after 20 minutes, add the basil stems, the remaining teaspoon of chilli flakes (for extra heat), half the basil leaves and the cherry tomatoes to the pan. Stir to combine and then lay the fish pieces over the top, well spread out. Make sure they are not submerged in the tomato and vegetable mix.

6. Return the pan to the oven for another 20 minutes to cook the fish. Garnish with the remaining basil and an extra crack of pepper. Serve with a side of rice or a lower-carb side salad.

Meal Prep

Separate portions of the tomato and vegetable mix into five sealed containers. If serving with rice, add a portion of rice to each container before adding the fish. Chill in the fridge for up to three days. To reheat, remove the fish fillet before microwaving the rest of the dish for one minute. Return the fish to the container and continue to cook for a further minute. This will prevent the fish from drying out.

Soy Marinated Eggs over Rice with Crispy Shallots

Veggie   Dairy Free

5 min prep + 20 min cook, plus 4–8 hr marinating

This recipe requires a little bit of prep, but the magic happens while you're going about your day. Soy marinated eggs are sooo rich in flavour and deliciously savoury. It takes staple cupboard ingredients and a little patience, but the result is worth the wait. Plus, eggs are one of the best cheap sources of protein around.

Serves 4

8 eggs
280 g white rice
5 tbsp soy sauce, plus extra to serve
1 tbsp rice vinegar
300 ml water
150 g kale, washed and roughly chopped
3 tbsp rapeseed oil
2 red chillies, finely chopped
1 tbsp peeled and finely grated fresh ginger
300 g shallots, thinly sliced
3 garlic cloves, crushed
chilli oil, to serve (optional)
salt and pepper to taste

Prep:

1. Set a pan of water over a medium heat and bring to the boil. Add the eggs, lower to a simmer and cook for seven minutes. Transfer the eggs to cold water to stop them cooking further. At the same time that the eggs are cooking, set another pan of water over a medium heat, bring to the boil, add the rice and cook for the amount of time given on the packet. Drain.

2. Meanwhile, add the soy sauce, rice vinegar and water to a large measuring jug. Remove the shells from the eggs and add them to the soy sauce mix. Place a small plate over the top of the eggs to ensure they remain submerged during the marinating process and chill in the fridge for a minimum of four hours (or for best results, eight hours).

3. Add the cooked rice to a separate container and chill in the fridge for up to two days. Freeze half the batch of rice if you want to eat it throughout the week.

When it's time to eat:

1. Preheat the oven to 220°C/200°C Fan. Line a baking sheet with parchment paper.

2. Pat the kale leaves dry with a clean tea towel and add to the baking sheet. Coat in one tablespoon of rapeseed oil and season generously with salt. Bake in the oven for 5–8 minutes, or until crispy.

3. Meanwhile, set a large frying pan or wok over a medium heat and add one tablespoon of rapeseed oil. Add the fresh chillies, ginger and 200 grams of the shallots to fry for two minutes before adding the garlic and cooked rice.

4. At the same time, set a separate pan over a medium heat, add the remaining rapeseed oil and the remaining 100 grams of shallots to fry until crispy.

5. To serve, add a portion of crispy kale and fragrant rice to each bowl. Slice two soy marinated eggs in halves or quarters and add, then drizzle over some of the marinade liquid and some additional soy sauce. Garnish with the crispy shallots and serve with a drizzle of chilli oil if you have a bottle in your cupboard.

Spiced Chicken Drumsticks with Roasted Veg & Couscous

5 min prep + 40 min cook

This recipe is inspired by Moroccan cuisine and its warming spices. Cinnamon gives the chicken a unique flavour that is so delicious and intriguing. You get to eat the rainbow with the array of veggies loaded into the dish, and thanks to the tasty and affordable spiced chicken drumsticks and the chickpeas, there's a high level of filling protein. I serve mine with couscous for a more authentic Moroccan feel, but rice would work as well. You could turn this recipe into a dinner party spread by pairing it with Moroccan-style sides such as hummus or a chopped spiced salad.

Serves 5

2 tsp smoked paprika
1 tsp ground cumin
1 tsp ground cinnamon
2 tbsp olive oil
1 kg chicken drumsticks, skin on
1 red pepper, seeded and
 roughly chopped
1 aubergine, roughly cubed
1 courgette, cubed
1 x 400 g can chickpeas, drained
 and rinsed
500 g couscous
650 ml chicken stock
5 tbsp natural yoghurt, to serve
salt and pepper to taste
handful of fresh parsley, torn,
 to garnish

Portion out the couscous into containers, followed by a layer of vegetables, chickpeas and the chicken and chill in the fridge for up to three days. When it's time to eat, reheat in the microwave on high for two minutes. Serve with a dollop of yoghurt and some fresh parsley.

1. Preheat the oven to 220°C/200°C Fan.

2. Add the spices to a bowl with the olive oil and mix together with some salt and pepper.

3. Take a large, deep baking sheet, add the chicken drumsticks and half the spiced oil and mix together to ensure the drumsticks are evenly coated. Cook in the oven for ten minutes.

4. Take a large bowl and add the red pepper, aubergine, courgette, chickpeas and the remaining spiced oil and stir until the vegetables are evenly coated.

5. Remove the chicken drumsticks from the oven after they have cooked for ten minutes, rotate the chicken and add the vegetable and chickpea mix to the baking sheet, filling in the gaps around the drumsticks. Return the baking sheet to the oven for 30 minutes.

6. Meanwhile, prepare the couscous. Add it to a large, heatproof bowl, pour over the just-boiled stock and cover with a lid to allow the couscous to soften for ten minutes.

7. To serve, dish up each portion of the hot couscous and top with some roasted vegetables and chickpeas and a couple of chicken drumsticks. Add a tablespoon of yoghurt on the side and garnish with fresh parsley leaves.

Weeknight Winners

Soy Pork Loins with Charred Cabbage Steaks

Low Carb High Protein Dairy Free

5 min prep + 15 min cook

This meal is a low-carb delight, packed with an umami punch. Perfect for a light dinner or lunch, paired with rice or noodles if you're feeling hungrier. Pork loins work so well as the centrepiece to this dish, as when coated with honey and soy sauce and then seared, you get the most delicious, sweet caramelisation and charring to the meat. If you haven't tried cabbage steaks yet, I hope this will be an introduction that gets you loving them. It's such a fun way to enjoy cabbage and personally I think it gives it the best texture. A hot tip for you: To make the spring onions look curly, like they are in the picture, add the thinly sliced pieces to a bowl of iced water.

Serves 5

5 pork loins
1 tbsp soy sauce
1 tbsp honey
2 tbsp rapeseed oil
1 white cabbage, cut into 2-cm thick steaks
100 ml water
pepper to taste
handful of fresh coriander, torn, to garnish

For the sauce
1 tbsp rapeseed oil
50 g spring onions, thinly sliced into strips
2 garlic cloves, crushed
5 tbsp soy sauce
1 tbsp honey
juice of ¼ lime, plus wedges to serve
400 ml cold water
4 tbsp boiling water
2 tbsp cornflour

1. Put the pork loins in a large bowl and add the soy sauce, honey and one tablespoon of the rapeseed oil, stirring to combine.

2. Meanwhile, preheat a frying pan over a high heat. Add the pork loins to the hot pan, frying them for around two minutes on each side until nicely charred and cooked through. Keep warm.

3. Using the same pan, add the remaining rapeseed oil and stir to take all the sticky bits off the bottom of the pan. Reduce the heat to medium/high and add the cabbage steaks with the water. Let it bubble away and cook the cabbage steaks for around three minutes on each side. Depending on the size of your pan, you may have to fry in batches of two or four.

4. Meanwhile, take a separate pan and prepare the sauce. Add the rapeseed oil, the whiter end of the spring onions and the garlic to the pan and set over a medium heat. Fry for a few minutes, before adding the soy sauce, honey, lime juice and cold water. Make a cornflour slurry by adding the hot water to the cornflour and mixing before adding to the sauce and heating until thickened. Either serve the sauce chunky, as it is, or pass through a sieve for a smoother sauce.

5. To serve, put a cabbage steak (or two depending on the size of your cabbage) on a plate. Slice up a pork loin and add on top of the cabbage, then spoon over some of the sauce and garnish with the remaining spring onions, coriander and a grind of pepper, plus a lime wedge alongside.

Lemon Chicken with Creamy Aioli Cabbage

Low Carb

10 min prep + 45 min cook

This is a refreshing, crunchy and creamy salad that you need to add into your weekly recipe rotation. When it comes to chicken in salad recipes, I always feel that roasted chicken thighs on the bone are often overlooked for chicken breast. Not only are the thighs the most reasonably priced cut of chicken, but you also get a crispy chicken skin topping and the most succulent meat to add to your salad. The dressing is inspired by aioli, using a garlicky, lemony mayo combination to tie all the ingredients together. I love to serve this dish as a weeknight dinner for friends, or it makes a great work-from-home lunch.

Serves 5

1.1 kg chicken thighs, skin on, on the bone
juice of ½ lemon, plus extra wedges to serve
1 tbsp olive oil
1 white cabbage, shredded
2 carrots, peeled into thin strips
1 red onion, thinly sliced
250 g radishes, halved and thinly sliced
salt and pepper to taste
large handful of fresh parsley, torn, to garnish

For the aioli
½ garlic clove, crushed
6 tbsp mayonnaise
juice of ½ lemon
salt and pepper to taste

1. Preheat the oven to 220°C/200°C Fan.

2. Put the chicken thighs on a baking sheet and add the lemon juice and olive oil and season with salt and pepper. Use your hands to ensure the chicken is evenly coated. Roast in the oven for 45 minutes until crispy and cooked, then set aside to cool.

3. For the aioli, first make a garlic paste by putting the crushed garlic clove half onto a chopping board with a pinch of salt. Use the side of a sharp knife to squish and drag the garlic until a paste is formed.

4. Take a large bowl (big enough to fit all the salad ingredients) and add the mayonnaise, garlic paste and lemon juice. Season with salt and lots of pepper.

5. Next, add the cabbage, carrots and red onion to the aioli dressing and mix together until incorporated.

6. When the crispy chicken thighs have cooled, remove the skin and remove the chicken meat from the bones. Shred the meat into bite-sized pieces and slice the crispy skin into strips.

7. To serve, add a bed of aioli salad mix to each bowl, a portion of the chicken pieces and crispy skin and finish with radishes and fresh parsley. Add a lemon wedge or two for squeezing over.

Air Fryer Preheat an air fryer to 190°C. Cook the chicken thighs for 25 minutes, starting skin-side down for the first ten minutes, then rotating and cooking skin-side up for the remaining 15 minutes.

Meal Prep

The firm nature of the vegetables in the salad means that this recipe is great for prepping ahead of time. Cook the chicken and chill in the fridge in its own sealed container until you need it. Prepare the salad elements and store together in a separate sealed container and prepare the dressing and store in a jar in the fridge. All ingredients will keep in the fridge for up to three days. If you want the chicken skin to crisp up again, pan-fry it for 2-3 minutes before serving.

Spinach & Artichoke Stuffed Courgette Boats

Low Carb **Veggie** **Gluten Free**

10 min prep + 30 min cook

This is one of my favourite low-carb meals to make and it requires minimal effort as the oven does most of the work for you. It's loaded with greens and cheesy flavours, making it a great dish to convince veggie haters/kids to increase their vegetable intake. Opt for mozzarella balls rather than pre-grated mozzarella as it's cheaper and (provided that you squeeze the moisture out before layering up the courgette boats) gives the best crispy, cheesy topping. Frozen spinach is also great here as it can be bulk bought for less and you won't have to rely on soggy spinach that has wilted at the back of your fridge when you want to make this recipe!

Serves 5

250 g frozen spinach
5 courgettes
1 tbsp olive oil
400 g cream cheese (2 packs)
juice of ½ lemon
90 g jarred artichokes, drained and roughly chopped
250 g mozzarella (2 balls), squeezed of excess liquid and torn into pieces
salt and pepper to taste

1. Preheat the oven to 220°C/200°C Fan.

2. Add the spinach to a bowl and cover with boiling water to defrost.

3. Slice the courgettes lengthways down the centre to give two halves or 'boats'. Use a teaspoon to remove the fleshy part of each courgette half to form a hollow area for the filling.

4. Using a pastry brush or your hands, coat the courgette hollows in olive oil and place on a baking sheet, cut-side up, before cooking in the oven for 15 minutes.

5. Meanwhile, drain the spinach and squeeze the excess moisture out with your hands (it should be cool enough by now). Add to a bowl with the cream cheese, lemon juice, artichokes and a pinch of salt and pepper. Stir well to combine.

6. Remove the courgettes from the oven and add around two heaped tablespoons of the spinach and cream cheese mix to each courgette half. Top each with a few pieces of torn mozzarella and a grind of pepper.

7. Return to the oven for a further 15 minutes, or until the cheese has melted and turned golden. Enjoy!

Air Fryer

Preheat an air fryer to 200°C and follow the same method as above, cooking the courgette boats in batches of four (depending on the size of your air fryer). Cook the hollow courgette boats for ten minutes, remove and add the fillings/toppings, then return to the air fryer to cook for a further ten minutes.

Creamy Chorizo & Corn Ditalini

Freeze

5 min prep + 20 min cook

This is one of my favourite recipes in the book. It incorporates such powerful flavours, while incorporating an array of fresh veggies that make this pasta dish 'chef's kiss'. Chorizo is, of course, the star of the show – not only is it a popular ingredient that packs a punch, but what is often ignored is how reasonably priced it is. What I love most about this meal is that the veg, meat and pasta are all similarly shaped into small pieces, meaning every mouthful is a pleasure.

Serves 5

1 tbsp olive oil
200 g chorizo, cubed
2 courgettes, diced
1 onion, diced
500 g frozen sweetcorn kernels
400 g ditalini
3 garlic cloves, crushed
½ tsp dried thyme
150 ml crème fraîche
large handful of fresh basil
  leaves, roughly chopped
salt and pepper to taste
2 tsp chilli flakes (optional)

1. Set a deep pan over a medium/low heat and add the olive oil, chorizo, courgettes and onion to fry. Season with salt and pepper and cook for ten minutes, stirring occasionally.

2. Meanwhile, put the sweetcorn in a heatproof bowl and defrost in the microwave for three minutes. Set aside.

3. Set a large pan of heavily salted water over a medium heat and bring to the boil, add the ditalini and cook for the amount of time given on the packet. Drain.

4. Meanwhile, add the garlic, thyme and defrosted sweetcorn to the chorizo pan and continue to fry until the pasta has cooked.

5. Transfer 250 millilitres of starchy pasta water to the chorizo pan. Also add a splash of pasta water to the crème fraîche and stir to temper it before adding it to the pan, along with the drained ditalini and two-thirds of the basil. Stir to combine.

6. To serve, spoon a portion of creamy chorizo ditalini into each bowl or plate, garnish with a few fresh basil leaves, a grind of pepper and a pinch of chilli flakes if you like some heat. Use a spoon to scoop maximum mouthfuls of flavour.

Meal Prep

Divide individual portions into sealed containers and chill in the fridge for up to three days. To heat up a serving, add one tablespoon of water before reheating in the microwave on high for two minutes. Stir to combine and garnish with some fresh basil if available.

Weeknight Winners

Aubergine Parmigiana

Freeze   Veggie

25 min prep + 30 min cook

Although this recipe takes a little more time and a few more pans than most, I promise it's worth the extra effort. Save for a cosy, rainy day as it's the ultimate comfort food, even though it's primarily made with veg. It's cheaper and lighter than a regular Parmigiana, as the mozzarella is reserved for the crispiest golden layer on top. Make it even more budget friendly by roasting stale bread with a little oil and blitzing in a food processor to form the toasty breadcrumb topping. I love to serve mine with a simple rocket side salad, but rice or warm greens would also be delicious.

Serves 5-6

2 tbsp extra virgin olive oil
1 onion, finely diced
4 garlic cloves, crushed
1 tsp dried oregano
2 x 500 g cartons passata
300 ml water
30 g fresh basil
2 tbsp rapeseed oil
3 or 4 large aubergines, cut into
   1-cm thick rounds
3 slices stale bread, blitzed to
   breadcrumbs
80 g Parmesan (opt for
   vegetarian if veggie), grated
250 g (2 balls) mozzarella,
   drained
salt and pepper to taste

1. Preheat the oven to 220°C/200°C Fan.

2. Set a deep, non-stick frying pan over a medium heat and add one tablespoon of the extra virgin olive oil and the onion. Season with salt and pepper and fry for about five minutes. Then add the garlic and dried oregano, fry for a further minute before adding the passata and water. Add half of the basil to the sauce and allow to simmer.

3. Meanwhile, set another frying pan over a high heat, add half a tablespoon of the rapeseed oil and fry a batch of the aubergine rounds for two minutes on each side until golden. The aubergine rounds must make full contact with the pan, so you may have to fry around four batches using half a tablespoon of rapeseed oil for each batch. It should take about 16 minutes in total.

4. While the sauce cooks and the aubergine is frying, add the breadcrumbs to a separate frying pan with the remaining extra virgin olive oil over a medium/low heat. Season with salt and pepper and fry until golden, stirring frequently to prevent burning.

5. Assemble the Parmigiana in an ovenproof dish, measuring around 25 cm x 25 cm. Spread two ladles of the tomato sauce across the base of the dish. Add a layer of aubergines, three tablespoons of breadcrumbs and three tablespoons of Parmesan, sprinkled evenly.

6. Repeat the process in step 5 for another layer. For the final layer, add a layer of aubergines, then the tomato sauce.

Meal Prep

If you want to make some of this ahead of time, you can do steps 1-8, cover with cling film and chill in the fridge for up to two days. When it's time to eat, bake for 30 minutes. For even quicker meal prep, bake for only five minutes with the foil removed in step 10. Divide portions into ovenproof sealed containers and chill in the fridge for up to four days or freeze for up to three months. When you're ready to eat, defrost overnight in the fridge and either reheat in the oven at 180°C/160°C Fan for 25 minutes or microwave on high for three minutes.

7. Prepare the mozzarella. Tear it into pieces and lay across one half of a clean tea towel. Pat dry with the other half of the tea towel and press lightly to remove the excess moisture.

8. Top the final layer of the Parmigiana with the dry, torn mozzarella and the remaining breadcrumbs.

9. Brush a light layer of olive oil over some foil to prevent sticking. Place over the dish, oil-side facing down and pop in the oven for 20 minutes.

10. Remove from the oven, take off the foil, then return to the oven for a further ten minutes until golden. Stand for two minutes, garnish with the remaining basil, then tuck in!

Tomato & Thyme Tart with Cream Cheese

Veggie

5 min prep + 25 min cook

This recipe is simple, delicious and gives a chance to show off your artistic flare. You can whip it up in around 30 minutes and once assembled, the oven does all the work. It's a fun way to get the kids involved in garnishing or flex your own garnishing skills and get creative with your tomato presentation. I love to serve this with a side salad – it's fresh tasting while still being comforting, and best of all, it has a short ingredients list which means less time spent shopping.

Serves 4

375 g (1 pack) ready-rolled puff pastry sheet
200–300 g cream cheese
juice of ½ lemon, plus extra wedges to serve
5 vine tomatoes, thinly sliced
1 tbsp extra virgin olive oil
½ tsp dried thyme
1 egg, beaten
salt and pepper to taste
small handful of fresh basil, leaves picked, to garnish

1. Preheat the oven to 210°C/190°C Fan. Line a baking sheet with parchment paper. Allow the puff pastry to reach room temperature if it has been stored in the fridge.

2. Add the cream cheese to a bowl and season with a generous amount of salt and pepper. Add the lemon juice and mix together, then set aside at room temperature.

3. Next, unroll the puff pastry and place on the prepared baking sheet. With a ruler and a knife, score a 2-cm border, ensuring you don't slice the whole way through the pastry. Using a fork, prick a few holes in the base to stop the centre puffing up when cooking.

4. Spread the cream cheese over the central area of the pastry leaving the outer border clear. Garnish with a layer of sliced tomatoes.

5. Mix the extra virgin olive oil, dried thyme and some salt and pepper in a bowl. Use a pastry brush to coat the tomatoes with the mixture. Clean the brush and then dip into the beaten egg and use to egg wash the pastry border.

6. Place the tart in the oven and cook for about 25 minutes until golden around the edges and the centre of the tart is cooked. I used a fork to poke the centre to feel if the base was firm.

7. Squeeze over a little lemon juice and scatter over the basil leaves to garnish. Season with salt and pepper and enjoy!

Buttermilk Roast Chicken with Smashed Potatoes

5 min prep + 1 hr 40 min cook
Plus 2 hr marinating

Note: *Depending on the weight of your chicken, adjust the cook time according to the packet time. Mine weighed 1.9 kg.*

I've used buttermilk as a marinade for chicken thighs so many times in preparation for making a burger or having a BBQ. It tenderises the meat beautifully, resulting in the most succulent chicken. So it got me thinking – a whole roast chicken is the most likely recipe to dry out – why not marinate it? I'm so pleased with the result as even the breast stays moist and tender when cooked in the buttermilk. Paired with smashed potatoes (crispy heaven) and root veg, roasted in the same tray so that they absorb all of the delicious chicken-y flavours, this recipe can't be beaten. Feel free to add any veg that is past its best to reduce waste, just be sure to add to the tray at the right time so that you don't under- or overcook it.

Serves 6

1.5–2 kg whole chicken
handful of fresh rosemary sprigs
300 ml buttermilk
2 tbsp olive oil
1 kg baby potatoes
500 g carrots, cut into thick strips
500 g parsnips, cut into thick strips
1 onion, cut into thick wedges
gravy, to serve (optional)
salt and pepper to taste
small handful of fresh parsley, roughly chopped, to garnish

1. Season the chicken with salt and pepper and place it in a large bowl with three sprigs of rosemary. Pour over the buttermilk and use your hands to massage the chicken, ensuring it is evenly covered. Place the chicken breast-side down so that the breast will get the most marinade. Pop in the fridge to chill for a minimum of two hours or overnight.

2. When you are ready to cook, remove the chicken from the fridge and allow it to come up to room temperature. Drain the buttermilk from the chicken. Use your hands to remove the excess buttermilk (parts that are dripping).

3. Preheat the oven to 210°C/190°C Fan.

4. Take a large roasting tray, add the olive oil, potatoes, carrots, parsnips, onion and four sprigs of rosemary. Season generously with salt and pepper and mix to ensure the oil, seasoning and vegetables are incorporated. Place the whole chicken on top of the vegetables and stuff any remaining rosemary into the cavity of the chicken. Form a dome of foil over the roasting tray and roast in the oven for one hour.

5. Remove the roasting tray from the oven, lift off the foil and the chicken and set aside. Use the bottom of a mug to press down on the potatoes, smashing them a little, then return the chicken to the baking sheet. Return to the oven for 40 minutes until golden, keeping an eye on the chicken to ensure it doesn't turn too dark brown. Loosely cover any parts with foil that brown too quickly to prevent the chicken from burning.

6. Remove the roasting tray from the oven and leave to stand for ten minutes. Loosely cover with foil to keep warm. Carve the chicken when you're ready to serve and assemble each plate of chicken, veggies and smashed potatoes. Pour over some gravy if you like and garnish with fresh parsley.

Halloumi Pasta

Freeze · Low Fat · Veggie

5 min prep + 25 min cook

This was my first recipe to 'blow-up' on Instagram. I think people were excited by it as it comes together in one pan, incorporates spice into the sauce and most importantly, is topped with halloumi. We're all used to topping pasta with cheese, but I think switching up your standard Cheddar or Parmesan with a crispy fried piece of tangy halloumi really elevates this dish to the next level.

Serves 5

1 tbsp olive oil
225 g low-fat halloumi cheese, thinly sliced
3–4 garlic cloves, finely chopped
1–2 red chillies, seeded (if preferred) and finely chopped
50 g spring onions, thinly sliced, reserving some of the greener ends for garnish
2 courgettes, 1 sliced into quarters, 1 grated
1 tsp smoked paprika
8 tbsp tomato purée
1.2 litres vegetable stock
400 g linguine
250 g cherry tomatoes, quartered
50 g green olives, pitted and thinly sliced
juice of ½ lemon
salt and pepper to taste
large handful of fresh basil, roughly torn
generous pinch of chilli flakes (optional)

1. Set a large, deep, non-stick frying pan over a medium/high heat and add half a tablespoon of the olive oil. Fry the halloumi slices on each side for two minutes, or until golden. Remove from the pan and set aside for later.

2. Add the remaining olive oil, the garlic, chillies and spring onions to the pan. Fry for a few minutes until fragrant.

3. Next, add the courgette quarters, paprika and tomato purée to the pan and season with salt. Fry for three minutes, then add the stock and linguine, bring to the boil and allow to bubble away for 12 minutes (stirring the pasta frequently to prevent sticking).

4. When the pasta is almost ready, add the tomatoes, olives, lemon juice and grated courgette to the pan and stir.

5. Top with the fried halloumi, the reserved (green) spring onions, the basil and extra fresh chilli. Season with a pinch of salt and pepper and devour! For an additional hit of heat, I also serve mine with a generous pinch of chilli flakes.

Five-ingredient Broccoli Mac 'n' Cheese

Freeze   Veggie

5 min prep + 20 min cook

This five-ingredient recipe is heavily influenced by American mac 'n' cheese. It's got a surprise ingredient – evaporated (unsweetened!) milk to replace the need for purchasing the multiple ingredients necessary for a roux. It prevents the dish from firming up too much as it cools, meaning that ten minutes after it's made, it remains as creamy and luxurious as when first cooked. This mac 'n' cheese is zero waste as I utilise the whole of the broccoli. You can also double the quantity of the broccoli for more of a loaded-vegetable-style dish. To balance the evaporated milk and maximise cheesiness, I suggest opting for extra-mature Cheddar.

Serves 5

300 ml cold water
1 large head of broccoli, stalks finely chopped, florets sliced into bite-sized pieces
500 g macaroni
1.2 litres boiling water
400 ml (unsweetened) evaporated milk
1 tbsp Dijon mustard
300 g extra-mature Cheddar, grated
salt and pepper to taste

1. Fill a large pan with the cold water and set over a medium/high heat. Bring to a simmer and add the broccoli stalks. Cook the stalks for five minutes until the water has evaporated.

2. Once the water has evaporated, add the macaroni, broccoli floret pieces and boiling water. Stir to combine, then simmer over a medium heat for ten minutes, stirring occasionally to prevent sticking.

3. When the pasta is almost cooked and the water almost completely evaporated, reduce the heat to low and add the evaporated milk, mustard and Cheddar. Season generously with salt.

4. Stir to combine and cook until the cheese has melted. Remove from the heat and grind over lots and lots of black pepper to serve.

Meal Prep Divide the pasta between five sealed containers and chill in the fridge for up to three days. To reheat, add one tablespoon of water and microwave on high for two minutes, stirring halfway. Season with lots of black pepper.

One-Pot Wonders

Nduja, Sausage & Mascarpone Pasta

Freeze

5 min prep + 25 min cook

This recipe is so deeply savoury and comforting - it's perfect when you want to whip up a zero-fuss pasta with maximum taste. The nduja, a Calabrian sausage paste, provides such an amazing, mildly spicy tang that pairs with the creamy mascarpone cheese so well. If you like sausages, then this one's for you, as the addition of browned sausage meat takes this to the next level. Combined with the rich, tomato-infused creamy sauce, each mouthful is heavenly. It's definitely a dish that makes it worth introducing nduja to your shopping list!

Serves 5

½ tbsp olive oil
8 pork sausages (450 g), casing removed and roughly torn
50 g spring onions, thinly sliced
200 g (1 tube) tomato purée
3 garlic cloves, crushed
3 tbsp nduja paste
1.1 litres chicken stock
500 g fusilli
150 g kale, washed and torn
100 g mascarpone cheese
salt and pepper to taste
pinch of chilli flakes (optional)

1. Set a deep, non-stick pan over a medium/high heat and add the olive oil and sausage meat. Distribute evenly across the pan and leave undisturbed for five minutes to brown. Season with salt and pepper. Transfer the sausage meat to a plate and set aside.

2. Next, add the white parts of the spring onions to the same pan and fry over a medium/low heat for two minutes before adding the tomato purée, garlic and nduja paste. Cook for six minutes until the tomato paste darkens (without burning).

3. Pour in the stock, add the browned sausage meat and bring to the boil. Add the fusilli to the pan and stir to combine.

4. Cover with a lid and simmer for ten minutes, stirring occasionally.

5. Next, add the kale and mascarpone cheese, stir to combine and cover with a lid. Cook for a further two minutes.

6. To serve, spoon a portion into each bowl, top with the greener ends of the spring onions and add a pinch of chilli flakes if you like some heat.

Meal Prep Divide the pasta between five sealed containers and chill in the fridge for up to three days. To reheat, add one tablespoon of water and microwave on high for two minutes, stirring halfway. Garnish with the reserved green spring onion ends.

Veggie Gnocchi Bolognese Bake

Freeze   Low Fat   Veggie

5 min prep + 40 min cook

Take one of the most well-loved, staple pasta sauces, switch it up and combine it with one of the most popular types of pasta and this pasta bake is born! It's such a simple yet delicious meal that is perfect to share with family and friends. By cooking the gnocchi in the sauce, the bolognese flavours infuse into the potatoey pillows, giving the best results. Plus, the cheese pull that you get when dishing up a portion is to die for. This recipe is veggie, but even if you're a meat-eater, I promise you won't miss the pork or beef. The depth of the base flavours with the lentils and soy sauce achieves a rounded, comforting bite that I believe rivals any classic bolognese.

Serves 5

2 tbsp olive oil
2 celery sticks, finely diced
1 large carrot, finely diced
1 onion, finely diced
4 garlic cloves, crushed
handful of fresh basil, stems
  finely chopped and leaves
  separated
1 tsp dried thyme
2 x 400 g cans plum tomatoes
200 g dried green lentils, rinsed
700 ml vegetable stock
1 kg (2 packs) gnocchi
250 g (2 balls) mozzarella,
  drained
1 tbsp soy sauce
salt and pepper to taste

1. Set a deep, ovenproof pan over a medium heat, add the olive oil, celery, carrot and onion and fry for seven minutes. Add the garlic, basil stems and dried thyme to fry for a further minute.

2. Add the plum tomatoes and use the back of a spoon to break them up before adding half of the basil leaves, the lentils and 500 millilitres of the stock. Simmer over a low/medium heat, partially covered with a lid (to allow some steam to escape) for 13 minutes. Stir occasionally as it cooks.

3. Add the gnocchi to the pan and the remaining 200 millilitres of stock, then leave to simmer for a further eight minutes, partially covered with a lid.

4. Preheat the grill to medium.

5. To remove the excess liquid from the mozzarella (which helps to maximise crispiness), roughly tear the ball into thin pieces and place on kitchen paper. Pat the mozzarella dry with another sheet of kitchen paper.

6. After the gnocchi has simmered for eight minutes, stir the soy sauce into the pan. Top with the mozzarella pieces and pop under the grill for 8–10 minutes, or until golden and crispy. Garnish with the remaining basil leaves and dish up!

Meal Prep

Divide the pasta into five containers, ensuring that the cheese is still on top. Chill in the fridge for up to three days. To reheat, place one tablespoon of water into the base of the container or heatproof bowl before microwaving for two minutes. Alternatively, place under a preheated grill for ten minutes.

One-Pot Wonders

Roasted Vegetable & Parmesan Orzo Bake

Freeze   Low Fat   Veggie

5 min prep + 1 hr cook

This recipe is like summer in a traybake. It's a loaded vegetable, cheesy, bright dish that is packed with Mediterranean vegetables and flavours. I love it as you can just throw everything into a roasting tray and let the oven work its magic. Although this dish has a slightly longer cook time than most, once you've chopped the vegetables and prepped the stock, you literally just have to open and close the oven door a few times while you enjoy a cocktail or two. Serve at a BBQ or meal prep to enjoy throughout the week.

Serves 5

2 courgettes, roughly cubed
1 aubergine, roughly cubed
3 mixed peppers, seeded and thinly sliced
1 red onion, cut into wedges
2 tbsp olive oil
1 tsp dried oregano
500 g orzo
handful of fresh basil leaves
2 tbsp tomato purée
3 garlic cloves, crushed
1.2 litres vegetable stock
juice of ½ lemon, plus wedges to serve
100 g Parmesan (opt for vegetarian if veggie), finely grated
salt and pepper to taste

1. Preheat the oven to 220°C/200°C Fan.

2. Add the vegetables, olive oil and dried oregano to a roasting tray and season generously with salt and pepper. Mix together to ensure everything is incorporated and place the tray in the oven for 30 minutes. After the first 15 minutes of cooking time, stir and tilt the tray, scooping out and discarding any excess liquid to maximise browning before returning to the oven.

3. After the full 30 minutes, remove from the oven and add the orzo and half the basil. Add the tomato purée, garlic and stock to a measuring jug and whisk together to combine, then pour over the orzo and vegetables. Stir and cover with foil. Return to the oven for 20 minutes.

4. After the cooking time, remove the tray from the oven and add the lemon juice and 50 grams of the Parmesan. Mix together to incorporate before sprinkling the remaining Parmesan over the top and returning to the oven for a final ten minutes, or until the top is golden and crispy.

5. Scatter over the remaining basil and any lemon wedges you have. Tuck in!

Meal Prep

Follow steps 1-3. Stir the lemon juice and half the Parmesan into the baking sheet of vegetables and pasta and divide the slightly undercooked orzo mix into five sealed containers. Chill in the fridge for up to three days or freeze for up to three months. When it's time to eat, defrost, then top with a sprinkle of Parmesan and either place under a hot grill for ten minutes or add one tablespoon of water to the container before reheating in a microwave on high for 2-3 minutes.

Stove-top Mushroom Lasagne

Freeze · **Low Fat** · **Veggie**

5 min prep + 30 min cook

I love lasagne for so many reasons, but one thing I don't enjoy is the amount of time and effort it takes to prepare. With this recipe, you get all the flavour and comfort of a regular lasagne and you only need to use one pan, the stove-top and 35 minutes of your time. There's a bit of therapeutic chopping involved, but trust me, the 'mushroom mince' is the perfect meat substitute. The mascarpone cheese saves the effort of making a roux and it's so good – I can't wait for you to try it!

Serves 5

2 tbsp olive oil
1 onion, finely diced
750 g mushrooms, finely chopped
2 tbsp tomato purée
1 tbsp fresh thyme leaves, plus extra small sprigs to garnish
3 garlic cloves, crushed
1 x 400 g can plum tomatoes
375 g lasagne sheets, broken in half
800 ml vegetable stock
125 g mascarpone cheese
50 g Parmesan (opt for vegetarian if veggie), finely grated
salt and pepper to taste

1. Set a large frying pan over a medium heat, add one tablespoon of the olive oil and the onion and sweat for around five minutes until the onion is translucent. Season with salt and pepper.

2. Add the mushrooms to the pan and continue to fry over a medium heat for around ten minutes until all the liquid is cooked off. The excess moisture must cook off to really maximise flavour, so don't rush this step!

3. Add the tomato purée, thyme leaves and garlic. Stir to deglaze the bits from the bottom of the pan and fry for two minutes.

4. Add the plum tomatoes (tip: before adding to the pan, use scissors to cut them up while in the can). Use the back of a spoon to break the tomatoes apart further and stir to combine. Season with salt and pepper and bring to a low simmer. Remove half the tomato mix and set aside in a heatproof bowl. Add a layer of halved lasagne sheets into the pan.

5. Return the reserved tomato mix to the pan, spooning it over the lasagne sheets, then roughly scatter the remaining lasagne sheet halves over the top. Pour over the stock. Ensure the lasagne sheets are submerged, but not touching the bottom of the pan, as you don't want them to stick. Put a lid on the pan and simmer for seven minutes.

6. Stir the contents of the pan and replace the lid. Cook for a further seven minutes, stirring occasionally to prevent sticking.

7. When all the liquids have been absorbed, add some swirls of mascarpone cheese and top with Parmesan and some sprigs of thyme. Season with lots of black pepper and dig in!

Meal Prep

Skip step 7 as you don't want to add the cheese until you're ready to eat. Divide the lasagne into five sealed containers and put in the fridge for up to three days. To reheat, microwave each portion with one tablespoon of water added on high for two minutes, stirring halfway. The sheets may break apart more, but it will still be delicious! Add a small swirl of mascarpone cheese and a sprinkle of Parmesan to serve.

Spicy Tomato Rice Topped with Halloumi & Coriander

Gluten Free · Low Fat · Veggie

5 min prep + 34 min cook

One of my most popular recipes to date. This is inspired by spicy Jollof-style rice as the rice is cooked in the stock and passata. Preparing it this way of course reduces the cleanup afterwards, but more importantly, it allows the flavour to infuse into the rice and vegetables. Halloumi is the best topping for this tomato rice – it balances out the spice and gives a salty kick with every bite. It's a popular recipe to meal prep, but you can also serve it to a crowd or cosy up and watch a film eating it.

Serves 6

2 tbsp olive oil
225 g halloumi cheese, thinly sliced
1 onion, finely diced
1 x 400 g can plum tomatoes
3 red chillies
3 garlic cloves, finely chopped
1 tbsp smoked paprika
3 tbsp tomato purée
500 g jasmine rice, rinsed thoroughly
800 ml gluten-free vegetable stock
600 g frozen mixed peppers, defrosted
200 g green beans, sliced into small pieces
salt and pepper to taste
large handful of fresh coriander, roughly chopped, to garnish
pinch of chilli flakes to taste (optional)

1. Set a large, deep frying pan over a medium/high heat and add one tablespoon of the olive oil. Fry the halloumi slices for two minutes on each side until golden. Remove from the pan and set aside for later.

2. Add the remaining tablespoon of oil to the same pan with the onion. Season with salt and pepper and fry over a medium/high heat for about six minutes until translucent.

3. While the onion is cooking, add the tomatoes and chillies to a blender and blitz until smooth. When the onion is ready, add the garlic, paprika and tomato purée and fry for a couple of minutes before pouring the blended tomato/chilli mix into the pan. Increase the heat for a further two minutes to heat the tomato mix through. Season with salt and pepper.

4. Reduce the heat and stir the rice and stock into the pan. Cover with a lid (or some foil if you don't have one) and reduce to a simmer for ten minutes.

5. Finally, add the mixed peppers (drained of any excess water) and green beans. Replace the lid or foil and cook for a further ten minutes.

6. When the spicy tomato rice is ready, serve with the fried halloumi on top, plus a sprinkle of coriander to garnish and chilli flakes for extra heat, if you like.

Ginger & Lime Chicken Legs with Coconut Rice

5 min prep + 50 min cook

This is one of my favourite recipes in the book. Not only is it one-pot, but it also requires minimal prep. I love how comforting a meal it is, yet every mouthful feels so fresh and vibrant, with the zingy ginger notes and the kick of lime, contrasting with creamy coconut rice.

Serves 5

1 tbsp rapeseed oil
5 chicken legs (about 1.1 kg), skin on
50 g spring onions, thinly sliced
4 garlic cloves, crushed
2 tbsp peeled and finely grated fresh ginger
350 g white rice, rinsed
750 ml gluten-free chicken stock
juice of ½ lime, plus wedges to serve
1 x 400 ml can coconut milk
100 g Tenderstem broccoli, florets sliced and stems thinly sliced
salt and pepper to taste
handful of fresh coriander, torn, to garnish

1. Set a deep frying pan over a medium heat and add the rapeseed oil. Season both sides of the chicken legs with salt and pepper, then place the legs skin-side down in the pan and leave to fry for around 15 minutes.

2. Rotate and cook the chicken legs for a further 15 minutes on the other side. The skin should be crispy and golden and the meat almost cooked through. Remove from the pan and set aside.

3. Add the spring onions to the same pan (reserving some of the greener ends for garnish) and add the garlic and ginger. Fry over a medium heat for a few minutes.

4. Add the rice to the pan and stir, then pour in the stock, lime juice and coconut milk.

5. Add the chicken legs back to the pan, skin-side facing upwards. Cover and leave to cook over a medium/low heat for 18 minutes, adding the broccoli after eight minutes.

6. Garnish with the reserved green spring onion ends, lime wedges and fresh coriander and dig in!

Separate portions of broccoli and coconut rice into five sealed containers along with a cooked chicken leg in each container. Chill in the fridge for up to three days or freeze for up to three months. If frozen, defrost in the fridge overnight. To reheat from chilled, heat in the microwave on high for two minutes. Top with the garnishes (stored separately) and enjoy!

One-Pot Wonders

Tomato, Sausage & Fennel Risotto

Freeze

5 min prep + 35 min cook

I believe this to be the gateway recipe for fennel haters everywhere – in fact, I used to detest fennel, but this dish is now one of my favourites in the book. Sausage and fennel is a combo that is often accompanied by pasta, but here I thought it would be great to add to a risotto. If you can't find risotto or arborio rice and want to make this recipe even cheaper, use standard long-grain rice and follow the same method. Meal prep for yourself to enjoy later in the week or serve to family and friends at a dinner party to impress fennel sceptics.

Serves 5

1 aubergine, roughly cubed
8 pork sausages (450 g), casing removed and roughly torn
1 tbsp olive oil
1 onion, finely diced
½–1 tsp fennel seeds
5 tbsp tomato purée
250 g cherry tomatoes, quartered
3 garlic cloves, crushed
375 g risotto or arborio rice
1.4 litres chicken stock
50 g Parmesan, finely grated, plus (optional) extra to serve
pinch of chilli flakes, to serve (optional)
salt and pepper to taste
handful of fresh parsley, finely chopped, to garnish

Meal Prep

Divide the risotto into five sealed containers and chill in the fridge as soon as the rice is cool for up to three days. Do not leave at room temperature for any amount of time once the rice has cooled.

1. Put the aubergine pieces into a colander, sprinkle over a few generous pinches of salt and massage into them. This will release and drain the bitter liquid from the aubergines while you prep the recipe.

2. Set a large, non-stick frying pan over a medium heat and fry the torn sausage meat. If you're using lean sausages, you can add a tiny bit of oil here, but most sausages should release enough fat to fry in. Leave undisturbed for five minutes to brown and then break apart into small pieces with the back of a spoon. Transfer the sausage meat to a plate and set aside (it doesn't need to be fully cooked at this point).

3. Add the olive oil and onion to the same pan and fry over a medium heat for three minutes. Season with salt and pepper.

4. Add the aubergine, fennel seeds (to taste), tomato purée and cherry tomatoes to the pan and fry everything for four minutes, stirring frequently.

5. Add the garlic and rice to the pan and leave to fry for a minute with the tomatoey sauce. Pour in a few ladles of stock and stir before leaving to simmer over a medium/low heat for a few minutes until the rice has absorbed the liquid.

6. Continue to add a few ladles of stock at a time while stirring frequently, repeating the process of adding more stock once the liquid has been absorbed. After around 20 minutes, when the rice is almost cooked, stir in the Parmesan, loosening with the last remaining ladles of stock.

7. When fully cooked, remove from the heat, then serve with an optional extra sprinkle of Parmesan and a pinch of chilli flakes if you like a touch of heat and fresh parsley to garnish.

Creamy Sun-dried Tomato & Pork Risotto

5 min prep + 45 min cook

Note: *If using frozen spinach, cover with boiling water for a minimum of five minutes, then drain and squeeze out any excess moisture before using in the risotto.*

This risotto is inspired by the flavours that are often found in creamy Tuscan pasta dishes. The sun-dried tomatoes impart such an amazing tartness that balances the creaminess of the sauce so well. Plus, you get the bonus of the delicious oil that they're stored in, saving you the need to use another oil from your cupboard. Using crème fraîche, a tangier option to cream, eliminates the need for another acid, like lemon, which makes this dish even more cost effective. If you can't find risotto or arborio rice and want to make this recipe even cheaper, use standard long-grain rice and follow the same method. It's a hearty, warming dinner that will comfort and relax, but is still packed with a good amount of nutrients.

Serves 5

2 tbsp sun-dried tomato oil (from the jar)
500 g pork mince
1 onion, finely diced
1 courgette, quartered lengthways and thinly sliced
100 g sun-dried tomatoes in oil, drained and thinly sliced
3 garlic cloves, crushed
375 g risotto or arborio rice
1.4 litres gluten-free chicken stock
150 g fresh or frozen spinach
handful of fresh basil leaves
150 ml crème fraîche or single cream
salt and pepper to taste

1. Set a large, non-stick frying pan over a high heat and add one tablespoon of the sun-dried tomato oil and the pork mince. Spread evenly across the pan and leave to brown for five minutes without stirring. After the five minutes, break the mince apart a little more and fry for a further three minutes. Set aside on a plate.

2. Next, reduce the heat in the same pan to medium and add the remaining sun-dried tomato oil and the onion. Season with salt and lots of pepper and gently fry for four minutes.

3. Add the courgette and sun-dried tomatoes and fry for a further 7–8 minutes.

4. Next, add the garlic and rice to the pan and leave to toast for a minute before adding a few ladles of stock. Stir and continue to cook over a medium/low heat for a few minutes until the rice has absorbed the stock.

5. Continue to add a few ladles of stock at a time while stirring frequently, repeating the process of adding more stock once the liquid has been absorbed. Add the browned pork mince halfway through.

6. After around 20 minutes, when the rice is almost cooked, add the spinach and half the basil leaves and allow to wilt. Stir in the crème fraîche and the last few ladles of stock. Remove from the heat. Top with the remaining basil leaves and lots of black pepper before serving in big bowls!

Meal Prep

Divide the risotto into five sealed containers as soon as the rice is cool and chill in the fridge for up to three days. Do not leave at room temperature for any time once the rice is cool. Add all the basil at the start of step 6 to ensure that none goes to waste.

Budget Seafood Paella

5 min prep + 35 min cook

This is my budget answer to one of the most well-known and well-loved Spanish dishes – Paella. It's not authentic as I don't use saffron to infuse or colour the rice, but instead use a tiny amount of turmeric (you can't taste it) which is more affordable and readily available in many homes. You'll be surprised to find that you can get 'frozen seafood cocktail' mixes in your supermarket for a reasonable price – they provide a variety of seafood which means that you don't have to buy lots of separate ingredients. I love serving this in the garden in the summer to friends and family, but it would also brighten up a dark winter's evening. My Spanish mum approves of this one, so I hope you do too!

Serves 6

1 tbsp olive oil
1 large onion, finely diced
1 red pepper, seeded and thinly sliced into small pieces
3 garlic cloves, crushed
2 tsp paprika
1 tsp ground turmeric
1 x 400 g can chopped tomatoes
500 g short-grain paella rice
900 ml gluten-free fish stock
200 g frozen peas, defrosted
300 g frozen seafood cocktail mix, defrosted
juice of ½ lemon, plus wedges to serve
salt and pepper to taste

1. Set a wide, shallow pan or paella dish over a medium heat, add the olive oil and onion and fry for four minutes. Season with salt and pepper.

2. Add the red pepper and fry for three minutes, adding the garlic and spices to the pan for the last minute. Stir together so the spices begin to bloom.

3. Add the tomatoes, then stir and fry over a high heat for three minutes until thickened.

4. Add the rice, stirring to incorporate everything, then pour in the stock. Season with salt and pepper and leave to simmer, without stirring, over a low/medium heat for 15 minutes.

5. Add the peas to cook for around four minutes, then add the seafood cocktail mix and lemon juice for the last few minutes, ensuring everything is heated through.

6. Leave the paella to stand for two minutes before serving with the lemon wedges around the circumference of the pan. Top with a good grind of black pepper and enjoy!

Red Lentil Dahl

Freeze · **Vegan**

10 min prep + 35 min cook

This nutritious dahl has been a favourite among my followers for a few years. It's such an easy one-pot dish that is ideal for meal prep as it freezes really well, and the flavours get better over time. It requires about ten minutes of prep and then you can put your feet up for 30 minutes. The spices have been simplified here compared to a more complex traditional dahl – grab any spices out of your cupboard for this flexible feast. I pair it with mini naans, but you can also serve it with rice if you prefer.

Serves 5

1 tbsp olive oil
2 onions, finely chopped
5 garlic cloves, crushed
40 g peeled and grated fresh ginger
large handful of fresh coriander, stalks finely chopped, leaves roughly chopped
3 carrots, sliced into thin moons
1 tsp ground cumin
1 tbsp curry powder
1 tsp ground turmeric
750 ml vegetable stock
1 x 400 g can chopped tomatoes
1 x 400 g can coconut milk
200 g dried red lentils, rinsed
juice of ½ lime, plus remaining wedges to serve
natural yoghurt, to serve (optional)
5 mini naans, to serve (or my Two-ingredient Flatbreads, see page 74)
salt to taste
pinch of chilli flakes per serving, to garnish

1. Take a large pan and set over a medium heat. Add the olive oil and a generous pinch of salt. Add the onions and gently fry for about 5–6 minutes or until they are translucent.

2. Then add the garlic, ginger, coriander stalks, carrots and spices. Fry for another two minutes before pouring in the stock, tomatoes, coconut milk and lentils.

3. Stir to combine, reduce the heat to a simmer and cook for 30 minutes. Add salt to taste.

4. Stir in the lime juice and serve each portion with an optional swirl of yoghurt. Garnish each with a sprinkle of chopped coriander leaves, a wedge of lime, a pinch of chilli flakes if you like, and serve with a mini naan on the side.

Slow Cooker

Add everything to the slow cooker and cook on high for three hours or on low for five hours.

Meal Prep

Portion the dahl into five sealed containers and chill in the fridge for up to three days. When it's time to eat, reheat in the microwave on high for two minutes while you toast your naan or flatbread.

Red Cashew Curry

5 min prep + 30 min cook

This vegan curry is so hearty and comforting. Ideal for a meatless Monday feast or as a meal prep recipe that can be divided into portions and frozen and enjoyed throughout the week. It's high in plant-based protein and you can adapt the spice level to your preference. Plus, if you haven't tried a cashew curry yet, you will soon be converted. The crunch, flavour and richness that the nuts provide when added to a curry are heavenly.

Serves 5

1 tbsp olive oil
1 onion, finely diced
4 garlic cloves, crushed
2 tbsp peeled and grated fresh ginger
2 red chillies, seeded and roughly chopped
1½ tbsp curry powder
6 tbsp tomato purée
1 aubergine, roughly cubed
1 litre gluten-free vegetable stock
1 x 400 ml can coconut milk
200 g dried red lentils, rinsed
100 g raw cashews
300 g frozen mixed peppers, defrosted
1 head of broccoli or 160 g Tenderstem broccoli
juice of ½ lime
white rice, to serve (optional)
salt to taste
handful of fresh basil, to garnish

1. Set a large pan over a medium heat, add the olive oil and onion and fry for three minutes. Season with salt.

2. Next, add the garlic, ginger, chillies, curry powder, tomato purée and aubergine. Fry over a medium heat, stirring continuously for two minutes.

3. Next, add the stock, coconut milk, red lentils and cashews and stir to combine. Cover with a lid and simmer over a low heat for 15 minutes.

4. After the mixture has cooked for the full amount of time, add the peppers and broccoli. Cook for a further ten minutes.

5. When the curry is ready, stir in the lime juice. Serve with rice, if you like, and top with some fresh basil leaves to garnish.

Throw all the prepped ingredients into the slow cooker, cover and cook on high for three hours or on low for five hours.

Portion out servings of curry into separate sealed containers and chill in the fridge for up to three days or freeze for up to three months. When it's time to eat, reheat a portion of curry in the microwave on high for two minutes. If cooking from frozen, defrost in the fridge overnight and ensure the rice isn't kept at room temperature for any time before microwaving.

Spiced Slow Cooker Chicken Noodle Soup

5 min prep + 3-4 hr cook

I love how low effort this soup is – throw everything into your slow cooker, walk away and let the ingredients work their magic. No slow cooker? No problem! Simmer over a medium/low heat for 40 minutes. It's a twist on standard chicken noodle soup as I add some spices and aromatics that give this recipe 'wow' factor. It makes so much sense to add spice to a dish that you'd often eat when feeling poorly. Chicken thighs with skin, on the bone, are not only the cheapest cut of chicken thigh, but also add a savoury depth of flavour to the soup. Once slow cooked, the tender meat tears straight off the bone – delicious and so convenient.

Serves 6

1.1 kg chicken thighs, skin on, on the bone
50 g spring onions, thinly sliced
1.5 litres chicken stock
250 g chestnut mushrooms, thinly sliced
1 tsp ground turmeric
2–3 carrots, peeled and thinly sliced into irregular pieces
6 garlic cloves, peeled and smashed
50 g fresh ginger, peeled and sliced
1 tsp chilli flakes (optional)
240 g spaghetti
juice of ½ lemon
salt and pepper to taste
handful of fresh dill, torn, to garnish

1. Pat the chicken thighs dry with kitchen paper and season with salt and pepper. Place into the slow cooker. Add the white ends of the spring onions, the chicken stock, mushrooms, turmeric, carrots, garlic and ginger. Add the chilli flakes if you like heat and season with salt and pepper.

2. Close the lid and cook for three hours on high or four hours on low.

3. During the last 20 minutes of cook time, add the spaghetti and lemon juice.

4. Remove the chicken thighs from the pot and, when cool enough to handle, discard the skin and tear the chicken meat from the bones, adding it back to the soup. Serve portions with a healthy sprinkle of fresh dill and a crack of black pepper. Simply remove the pieces of garlic and ginger that were infusing the soup as you come across them while you eat, if you like.

Love it or Hate it Spaghetti

Low Fat · Veggie

2 min prep + 10 min cook

Note: *Increase or decrease the quantity of yeast extract spread depending on your preference. I go for three tablespoons, but I love it stroooong.*

This recipe is a flavour powerhouse, using only three ingredients. It's one for the Marmite lovers, and those people will know that salty Marmite and cheese is a winning combination. Why not take these key ingredients and create a low effort, high reward pasta dish. Pair it with some greens and a protein to make it a balanced meal or enjoy as a speedy hangover cure or dinner treat when you're feeling lazy.

Serves 4

400 g spaghetti or linguine
80 g Parmesan (opt for vegetarian if veggie)
2–3 tbsp yeast extract spread (I use Marmite)
salt to taste

1. Set a large pan of salted water over a medium heat and bring to the boil. Add the pasta and cook for two minutes less than the packet cooking time.

2. Meanwhile, finely grate the Parmesan cheese.

3. When the pasta is cooked, reserve 400 millilitres of the pasta water before draining.

4. Transfer the pasta back to the pan over a low heat along with 300 millilitres of the reserved pasta water and the yeast extract spread.

5. Use tongs to quickly stir the mixture, gradually adding the Parmesan while stirring vigorously to form a cheesy sauce. Continue to heat gently until the sauce thickens, loosening with the remaining 100 millilitres of pasta water if necessary. Time to eat!

Goats' Cheese, Spinach & Basil Linguine

2 min prep + 10 min cook

This vibrantly green pasta recipe is one of my favourites in the book. Not only is it bright and Instagrammable, it's also so delicious. The frozen spinach is reasonably priced and you don't have to worry about it going off in the fridge. And the goats' cheese provides creaminess, acidity and tang, all in one ingredient (hello, cost effective!). This is ideal for a speedy meal when you're in a rush, or to serve to friends at a dinner party when you don't want to spend half the night in the kitchen.

Serves 5

1 tbsp olive oil
1 onion, diced
500 g linguine
3 garlic cloves, finely grated
160 g frozen spinach
125 g goats' cheese
30 g fresh basil
salt and pepper to taste
chilli flakes (optional)

1. Set a non-stick pan over a medium heat and add the olive oil. Add the onion, season with salt and pepper and gently fry for four minutes.

2. Meanwhile, set a large pan of salted water over a medium heat and bring to the boil. Add the linguine and cook for two minutes less than the packet cooking time.

3. While the pasta is cooking and once the onion has softened, add the garlic to fry for a minute before adding the frozen spinach to the pan, along with 400 millilitres of the starchy pasta water. Increase the heat and cook the spinach and onion mix until the pasta is ready.

4. Add the spinach and onion mix to a blender with half the goats' cheese and the basil and blitz until smooth.

5. Drain the linguine and transfer back to the pan. Pour over the blended sauce and continue to cook over a low/medium heat.

6. After about two minutes, the sauce should thicken and coat the linguine. Serve with a sprinkle of the remaining goats' cheese and a pinch of salt and pepper. Top with chilli flakes if you love a little heat.

Cacio e Pepe Gnocchi

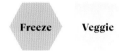

2 min prep + 6 min cook

Take one of the most famous Roman pasta dishes and combine it with one of the most delicious and comforting types of pasta and Cacio e Pepe Gnocchi is born. This recipe uses minimal ingredients and yet the flavour is so complex and rich. Traditional cacio e pepe is made with Pecorino cheese, however, I have opted for the more budget-friendly Parmesan, which is just as flavoursome.

Serves 4

1 kg (2 packs) gnocchi
1 tbsp coarsely ground black pepper
50 g butter
100 g Parmesan (opt for vegetarian if veggie), finely grated
salt and pepper to taste

1. Set a large pan of heavily salted water over a medium heat and bring to the boil. Add the gnocchi and cook for one minute less than the packet cooking time.

2. Meanwhile, set a non-stick pan over a medium heat and add the coarsely ground black pepper. Toast for two minutes.

3. Next, add the butter to the toasted pepper in the pan and heat until melted. Transfer 150 millilitres of starchy pasta water to the pan and stir to combine.

4. Reserve an extra mugful of the starchy cooking water before draining the gnocchi and transferring it to the pan. Stir to combine the gnocchi and buttery pepper mix and gradually add the Parmesan to the pan while stirring continuously over a low heat.

5. Continue to heat until the sauce has thickened and the Parmesan has melted. Loosen with some of the reserved starchy water as necessary. Enjoy immediately with an extra grind of pepper and a pinch of salt.

Turkey Steaks with Peppercorn Sauce & Greens

Low Fat · Low Carb · High Protein · Freeze

5 min prep + 15 min cook

I love that turkey steaks are a more budget-friendly, yet super tasty answer to a standard beef steak. You can often buy them in packets of four, making them really economical as a centrepiece for a family meal. I've paired the steaks with a fiery, peppery sauce and fresh leeks and peas as a low-carb dinner or lunch that you can whip up in a short amount of time. Vibrant peas and silky, buttery leeks provide the fibre, keeping you fuller for longer, but you could easily add mash or rice if you want to make this meal high carb.

Serves 4

500 g leeks, thoroughly washed and thinly sliced
200 g frozen peas
1 tbsp butter or olive oil
2 tbsp rapeseed oil
4 turkey steaks, 375 g total weight
1 onion, finely diced
1 tbsp coarsely ground black pepper (or ½ tbsp finely ground pepper)
3 garlic cloves, crushed
800 ml beef stock
150 ml single cream
2½ tbsp cornflour
4 tbsp boiling water
salt and pepper to taste

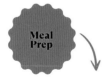

Meal Prep

Store the sauce, turkey steaks, leeks and peas separately in sealed containers in the fridge for up to three days. When it's time to eat, microwave the leeks and peas and turkey steaks in a heatproof bowl on high for two minutes. Reheat a serving of sauce in a mug in the microwave on high for 30 seconds. Pour over and enjoy!

1. Take a heatproof bowl, add the leeks and frozen peas and cover with a small plate. Microwave on high for 5–8 minutes, adding the butter/olive oil and a pinch of salt and pepper halfway through the cooking time. Stir occasionally.

2. Meanwhile, set a frying pan over a high heat, add one tablespoon of the rapeseed oil, then add the turkey steaks and fry on each side for two minutes. Set aside.

3. Reduce the heat to medium and add a splash of water to deglaze the pan, scraping any brown bits off the bottom. Add the remaining rapeseed oil, the onion, coarsely ground pepper and a pinch of salt to the pan to gently fry for five minutes until the onion has softened. Add the garlic for the final minute of cooking time.

4. Next, reduce the heat to low before adding the beef stock and the cream. The heat should not be too high otherwise the cream will split.

5. Take a small bowl and add the cornflour and the boiling water, stirring well to form a cornflour slurry. Pour into the pan and increase the heat. Stir and heat the cream and cornflour mix until thickened.

6. To serve, either plate up the turkey steaks whole, or slice into strips and serve with a portion of leeks and peas. Pour over the creamy peppercorn sauce and dig in!

Fish Finger Burrito

5 min prep + 12 min cook

Fish fingers are the most underrated food. They're great in sandwiches, served with chips, topped on pasta, stuffed in tacos and in burritos. The crispy battered protein is ready in under 12 minutes and gives the ideal texture and flavour for this full-to-the-brim burrito. Trust me on this one, try it once and it'll be in your weekly recipe rotation in no time.

Serves 5

20 frozen fish fingers
400 ml water
150 g white rice, thoroughly rinsed
6 tomatoes, finely diced
1 red onion, finely diced
30 g fresh coriander, roughly chopped
juice of 1 lime
4 small, ripe avocados, peeled and stoned
5 large wraps
1 x 400 g can black beans, drained and rinsed
salt and pepper to taste

1. Preheat the grill to medium or the oven to 220°C/200°C Fan.

2. Cook the fish fingers for 12 minutes, or until golden and crispy.

3. Meanwhile, set a pan filled with the water over a medium heat and bring to a simmer. Add the rice and cook for the time given on the packet instructions. Drain.

4. In a bowl, combine the diced tomatoes, red onion and coriander to make a simple pico de gallo (tomato salsa). Add the juice of half a lime and season generously with salt and pepper.

5. In another bowl, mash the avocados along with the juice of the other lime half. Season with salt and pepper.

6. To serve each burrito, take one of the wraps and add a dollop of avocado to the centre. Next, add a layer of rice, some black beans, a spoonful of tomato salsa and four crispy fish fingers.

7. Fold the sides of the burrito inwards before tightly rolling away from you. Tuck in and enjoy!

Air Fryer

To reduce energy use, cook your fish fingers in the air fryer. Preheat to 200°C and cook for eight minutes, rotating halfway.

Mini Spiced Halloumi Wraps

5 min prep + 7 min cook

Note: *If you have any spare baby gem lettuce or cabbage mix, you can enjoy it as a side salad with a drizzle of leftover dressing.*

This recipe was the first time I experimented with coating halloumi cheese in curry powder and wow, now it's the only way I want to enjoy halloumi. The flavour combination is dreamy and when paired with a refreshing salad and a tangy sauce, all encased in a tasty wrap, it makes for the best speedy lunch. Purchasing the pre-made cabbage mix or coleslaw cuts the cost as you don't have to individually buy the white cabbage, red cabbage and carrots for the slaw and it saves you time.

Serves 4

2 tsp curry powder
1 tbsp rapeseed oil or olive oil
225 g halloumi cheese, sliced into 1-cm strips
200 ml natural yoghurt or mayonnaise
juice of ½ lime
8 mini wraps
2 heads of baby gem lettuce, washed and sliced
275 g cabbage mix or coleslaw
salt and pepper to taste
small handful of fresh mint, leaves picked and roughly chopped (optional)

1. Add the curry powder and rapeseed oil to a bowl and stir to combine. Add the halloumi strips to the bowl and coat in the curry powder oil.

2. Preheat a griddle pan over a medium/high heat, place the halloumi strips into the pan and fry for about two or three minutes on each side until golden and crispy.

3. Meanwhile, for the dressing, combine the yoghurt with the lime juice, a pinch of salt and lots of pepper. (Use the juice from a quarter of a lime if you like less tang.)

4. Take a mini wrap, add a layer of sliced lettuce and a serving of cabbage mix. Drizzle over some creamy, tangy yoghurt dressing and top with some of the spiced halloumi strips. Garnish with a little of the chopped mint leaves, if you like. Fold the wrap over before devouring. Repeat the layering process for each wrap.

Tuna Rice Bowl with Crispy Cavolo Nero

5 min prep + 12 min cook

This is my budget take on the salmon and rice bowl that has gone viral. Canned tuna is one of the best affordable sources of protein, so I often try to incorporate it into my recipes. When considering how I could put my own spin on this popular viral recipe, tuna seemed like the best substitute for salmon as it not only costs less, but also reduces any effort and cook time without forfeiting on flavour. I've opted for crispy salted cavolo nero, which when roasted acts as an amazing budget alternative to sushi nori.

Serves 4

300 g white rice, rinsed
 thoroughly
150 g cavolo nero, leaves
 removed from stems
1 tbsp olive oil
4 x 145 g cans tuna in brine,
 drained
juice of 1 lime, plus 1 lime, cut
 into quarter wedges to serve
4 tbsp mayonnaise
2 tbsp sriracha
50 g spring onions, thinly sliced
small handful of fresh coriander,
 roughly torn
salt and pepper to taste

1. Preheat the oven to 200°C/180°C Fan. Line a baking sheet with parchment paper and set aside.

2. Set a pan of water over a medium heat and bring to the boil. Add the rice and simmer for the amount of cooking time given on the packet.

3. Meanwhile, tear the cavolo nero leaves into large pieces and place in a bowl. Coat the leaves in the olive oil and add a generous pinch of salt. Mix thoroughly with your hands, transfer to the prepared baking sheet and pop in the oven for 6–8 minutes, checking occasionally to ensure the cavolo nero does not burn.

4. Once cooked, drain the rice and add to a large bowl. Add the tuna and lime juice, then season with salt and pepper and stir to combine.

5. For each serving, take a bowl and portion out a generous helping of the rice mix. Drizzle over one tablespoon of the mayonnaise and half a tablespoon of the sriracha. Place a portion of cavolo nero to the side of the bowl and finish with the spring onions, coriander and a wedge of lime. Use the crispy cavolo nero to scoop up the delicious rice as you dig in!

Miso Noodle Bowls

5 min prep + 2 min cook

This was my first recipe on TikTok to get 100k likes. I think it was so popular because it's the solution to a rushed lunch without compromising on flavour or nutrients. You can assemble the bowls ahead of time, making it a super-easy meal prep recipe and it's easily customisable. Why not mix up your favourite veggies or add a protein source if you want to make it more substantial? The warming miso-infused broth is comforting and pairs beautifully with the soft noodles.

Serves 5

250 g mushrooms, thinly sliced
2 heads of pak choi, stems thinly
   sliced, leaves sliced into strips
250 g rice noodles
25–50 g spring onions, thinly
   sliced
2½ vegetable stock cubes
5 tbsp (heaped) miso paste
2 litres boiling water
5 tbsp soy sauce
5 tbsp rice vinegar (optional)
lime juice to taste (optional)

1. Take five meal prep containers, add to each a serving of the mushrooms, pak choi, rice noodles, spring onions, half a stock cube and one heaped tablespoon of the miso paste.

2. Seal each container and chill in the fridge for up to four days.

3. When you're ready to eat, empty the contents of a meal prep container into a heatproof bowl and add 400 millilitres of boiling water. Add one tablespoon of the soy sauce and one tablespoon of the rice vinegar, if using, and cook in the microwave on high for two minutes.

4. Add a squeeze of lime juice, if you like, stir and enjoy!

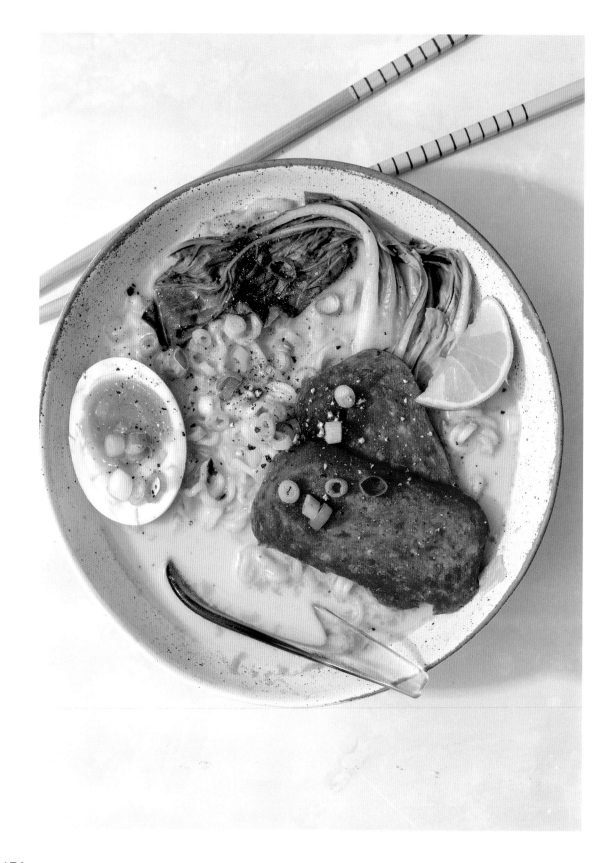

Instant Pork Ramen

4 min prep + 6 min cook

Note: *When choosing which instant noodles to buy, purchase a packet that is intended for making a brothy noodle dish instead of one where the noodles aren't in any liquid. I'd also opt for a spicy pack to flavour the creamy broth.*

This is the quickest comfort meal you'll ever make. For ten minutes of effort you'll get major flavour and a dish that feels like a takeaway. This recipe is inspired by the Japanese Tonkotsu – a type of ramen served in an amazing creamy-ish broth. It's usually topped with pork belly which I have tried to emulate with canned pork and ham to keep it within budget. You might be sceptical about meat that's come out of a can, but trust me on this one, it's so flavourful and acts as the best topping.

Serves 4

1 tbsp rapeseed oil
200 g canned pork and ham (I use Spam), sliced into thin planks
800 ml milk
1.2 litres water
4 x 70 g packs instant noodles, seasoning sachets reserved
2 heads of pak choi, sliced lengthways into quarters
2 eggs (optional)
handful of spring onions, thinly sliced
1 lime, cut into wedges to serve
pepper to taste

1. Set a non-stick frying pan over a medium heat and add the rapeseed oil. Add the meat to the pan and fry for three minutes on each side until golden and crispy.

2. Meanwhile, set a deep pan over a medium heat, add the milk and water and bring to a low simmer. Add the noodles, ensuring they are all submerged. Add the pak choi and cover with a lid, simmering for the cooking time given on your noodle packet.

3. Meanwhile, if using eggs, set a pan of water over a medium heat and bring to the boil. Gently lower the eggs into the water, cook for six minutes, then transfer to a bowl of cold water to stop them from cooking any further.

4. When the noodles and pak choi are ready, add any seasoning sachets to the pan and stir to combine.

5. Remove the shells from the eggs and slice each in half. Serve each portion of ramen in a deep bowl, ladling in some of the broth, a serving of noodles and pak choi, a couple of slices of meat and half a jammy egg. Sprinkle over some crunchy spring onions to finish. Add a lime wedge and a generous grind of pepper before digging in!

Tofu Laksa Curry

3 min prep + 12 min cook

Note: *For the crispiest tofu, press as much moisture as you can out of it before cooking. Place on a clean tea towel to absorb any excess moisture.*

This tofu curry uses supermarket branded Laksa paste, my favourite type of curry paste. It's so fragrant, mild and delicious and creates the perfect shortcut to Flavourtown. More traditional Laksa curries are topped with an egg and paired with either chicken, pork or prawns. I've switched it up and gone for tasty tofu which I love to use as an affordable vegetarian protein. The crispy cornflour batter takes tofu to another level, making this speedy dinner feel even more special.

Serves 5

2 tbsp rapeseed oil
5 garlic cloves, thinly sliced
180 g frozen green beans
4 tbsp Laksa paste
1 x 400 ml can coconut milk
1 litre vegetable stock
200 g beansprouts
400 g firm tofu, pressed and cubed
2 tbsp cornflour
250 g rice noodles
1 lime, cut into wedges to serve
salt to taste
small handful of fresh coriander leaves (optional)

1. Set a non-stick frying pan over a medium heat, add one tablespoon of the rapeseed oil and the garlic and gently fry for about four minutes until golden and crispy to form the 'garlic chip' topping. Set the garlic aside and season with salt. Reserve the garlic oil in the pan.

2. Meanwhile, add the green beans to a heatproof bowl and defrost for two minutes in the microwave. Chop into bite-sized pieces once cooled and set aside.

3. Add the Laksa paste to the garlic-infused oil in the pan and stir over a medium heat for one minute before adding the coconut milk, vegetable stock, green beans and beansprouts. Increase the heat slightly to bring to a low simmer for eight minutes.

4. Put the tofu cubes in a bowl, add the cornflour and toss to coat evenly.

5. Meanwhile, set another non-stick frying pan over a medium heat and add the remaining rapeseed oil. Add the tofu cubes and fry them, spaced well apart in the pan, for about two minutes on each side until golden. Season generously with salt once cooked and set aside.

6. Meanwhile, add the rice noodles to a large, heatproof bowl and cover with boiling water.

7. After eight minutes, drain the noodles and divide between bowls to serve. Ladle over the Laksa curry, top with the crispy tofu and reserved garlic chips, add a lime wedge and garnish with some coriander leaves, if you like.

Peanut Noodles with Quick Pickled Cucumber

Veggie **Freeze**

5 min prep + 15 min cook

You'll be surprised at how much flavour can be whipped up in 15 minutes with this dish. A rich, nutty sauce is balanced with zingy pickled cucumber and it's ideal to share with friends or family, or to use as a meal prep recipe. The foundation of the sauce is made with staple cupboard ingredients, so it's a great choice when you don't know what to cook as you can easily adapt the veg according to what needs using up in your fridge.

Serves 5

For the pickled cucumber
1 tsp chilli flakes, plus (optional) extra to garnish
1 tbsp rice vinegar
1 tsp sugar
1 whole cucumber, thinly sliced
salt to taste

For the noodles
1 tbsp rapeseed oil
250 g chestnut mushrooms, thinly sliced
160 g mangetout
3 garlic cloves, finely grated
1 tbsp peeled and grated fresh ginger or 1 tsp ground ginger
50 g spring onions, thinly sliced
200 g egg noodles (4 nests)
4 tbsp peanut butter
600 ml vegetable stock
2 tbsp soy sauce
1 tbsp rice vinegar
75 g honey roasted peanuts, roughly chopped, to garnish

1. Start by making the pickled cucumber. To a bowl, add the chilli flakes, rice vinegar, sugar, a pinch of salt and the cucumber slices. Stir to combine and set aside to pickle.

2. For the noodles, set a large, non-stick pan over a high heat, add the rapeseed oil and mushrooms. Brown the mushrooms for five minutes without stirring.

3. When the mushrooms have taken on some colour, stir and then add the mangetout. Cook for a further three minutes before reducing the heat and adding the garlic, both gingers and the white ends of the spring onions. Cook for two minutes.

4. Meanwhile, set a pan of water over a medium heat and bring to the boil, add the noodles and cook for the amount of time given on your packet.

5. Add the peanut butter and 100 millilitres of the vegetable stock to the mushroom and mangetout pan to loosen and stir until smooth. Add a further 400 millilitres of the vegetable stock, the soy sauce and rice vinegar to form a sauce. Continue to cook while the noodles are boiling.

6. Drain the noodles and add to the pan with the peanut sauce. Stir to combine and loosen with the remaining 100 millilitres of stock. Serve in bowls. Garnish each serving with the green spring onion tops, a sprinkle of roasted peanuts, pickled cucumber and some chilli flakes if you like some heat.

Meal Prep

Follow steps 1, 2, 3 and 5, making the sauce ahead of time. Store the sauce in sealed containers in the fridge for up to four days. When you're ready to eat, cook one serving of noodles, drain and add to the pan with a serving of sauce. Stir to combine and loosen with a little water if needed. Reheat until hot. Serve with the toppings.

BLT Stacked Bagel

High Protein

5 min prep + 10 min cook

This recipe takes a BLT - that classic, well-loved bacon, lettuce and tomato combo - and throws in an element of the grinder salad sandwich that went viral. This dish has a tangy, creamy, seasoned lettuce filling that, I think, takes this BLT to the next level. Oh, and it's served up in a bagel because bagels are chewy and robust enough to hold a fully loaded filling. This is ideal as a quick work-from-home lunch, which has the added bonus of the leftover salad acting as a side dish.

Serves 5

300 g (10 rashers) back bacon rashers (I prefer smoked)
1 iceberg lettuce, shredded
5 tbsp mayonnaise, plus extra for spreading
20 jarred jalapeño slices, plus 1 tbsp brine
1 tsp dried oregano
5 bagels (I love seeded)
1 whole cucumber, thinly sliced
1 red onion, sliced into thin rings
6 salad tomatoes, thinly sliced
salt and pepper to taste

Air Fryer

Preheat the air fryer to 200°C and add the bacon to the air fryer basket with a drizzle of oil. Cook for eight to ten minutes, or until until crispy.

1. Set a non-stick frying pan over a low heat and add the bacon. Fry for five minutes without touching the bacon to allow the fat time to render.

2. Meanwhile, prepare the salad. Take a large bowl, add the lettuce, mayonnaise, one tablespoon of jalapeño brine, the dried oregano and salt and pepper to taste. Stir to combine and set to one side.

3. Once the bacon has rendered its fat, increase the heat slightly and rotate. Fry for a further five minutes. Once crispy, transfer the bacon to a plate lined with kitchen paper to absorb some of the excess fat and set aside.

4. To serve, slice each bagel in half, then toast. Remove any visible fat from the bacon. Add a layer of creamy lettuce to one toasted bagel half, a few slices of cucumber, two rashers of bacon, a few slices of red onion and tomato and four jalapeño slices. Spread a small amount of extra mayonnaise onto the remaining toasted half of the bagel and assemble.

5. Wrap in parchment paper and slice in half – the paper will help hold the bagel halves together and keeps the filling in place as you take your first bite.

Tuna Brie Melt

Freeze   High Protein

4 min prep + 6 min cook

When deciding on how I could put my own spin on a classic tuna melt, I knew that I wanted to get experimental with the cheese. Brie is surprisingly cheap when compared to so many other gooey cheeses such as Gruyère or Fontina. It strikes the perfect rich note against the salty tuna and I hope it will become your new fave sandwich combo. Such an easy treat for lunch that will almost certainly brighten your day. Fresh herbs really up the taste factor in this sandwich. You can add parsley or basil instead of the dill if you prefer so you don't have to miss out!

Serves 5

4 x 145 g cans tuna (in brine),
   total drained weight of 400 g
50 g spring onions, thinly sliced
7 tbsp mayonnaise
small handful of dill, finely
   chopped
10 slices seeded brown bread
5 tsp Dijon mustard
300 g Brie, sliced into planks
salt and pepper to taste

1. Take a large bowl and add the tuna, spring onions, four tablespoons of the mayonnaise and the dill. Season with salt and pepper and stir to combine.

2. To make each sandwich, take two slices of bread. Spread one slice of bread with one teaspoon of the mustard and spread about half a tablespoon of mayonnaise on the exterior sides of both pieces of bread. This will result in the crispiest texture.

3. Take the slice of bread spread with mustard and add a few slices of Brie to it. Then add a generous layer of the tuna mix and top with the other slice of bread, ensuring the mayonnaise is on the outside of the sandwich.

4. Set a non-stick frying pan over a medium heat and cook the sandwich for three minutes on each side until lightly browned.

5. Slice in half and get lost in the cheesiest tuna melt that you've ever tasted.

Air Fryer

Preheat an air fryer to 190°C and add the sandwich. Cook for three minutes, then rotate and cook for a further three minutes until golden and crispy.

Crispy Chilli Chicken

5 min prep + 15 min cook

Note: *A cornflour slurry is a mix of cornflour and boiling water. The cornflour dissolves in the boiling water to form a thick 'slurry' which prevents clumping when added to the pan.*

This recipe is inspired by one of the most popular dishes at a Chinese takeaway: crispy fried chicken. Traditionally, the chicken is deep-fried, often with the addition of MSG and other flavourings. I have made a few adaptations here to reduce the amount of oil and simplify the dish. The chicken is shallow-fried and coated in a spicy soy/honey sauce that will have you going back for more. You can adapt the heat level by adjusting the type and quantity of chillies. Serve with rice and green beans to make this a main or simply enjoy as a side with your friends and family.

Serves 5

650 g boneless, skinless chicken thighs, sliced into thin chunks
1 egg, lightly whisked
3½ tbsp cornflour
2–3 tbsp rapeseed oil
300 g green beans
250 g white rice
2–3 garlic cloves, crushed
2 red chillies, 1 finely chopped and 1 thinly sliced
1½ tbsp sweet chilli sauce
4 tbsp soy sauce
1½ tbsp cornflour, plus tbsp boiling water, mixed
juice of ½ lime, remaining wedges to serve
50 g spring onions, thinly sliced, to garnish

1. Place the chicken pieces in a large bowl. Add the egg to the bowl and evenly coat the chicken, then stir in the cornflour until each piece is covered in the light batter.

2. Set a large, non-stick frying pan over a high heat, add one tablespoon of the rapeseed oil and fry the pieces of chicken in batches, rotating after about four minutes to ensure each chunk is golden and crispy. Add more rapeseed oil before frying each batch and then set to one side once all the chicken has been cooked.

3. Meanwhile, steam or boil the green beans. Put the rice on to cook according to the packet instructions. Drain.

4. Using the same pan you cooked the chicken in, reduce the heat and add the garlic and finely chopped chilli. Fry for a couple of minutes before adding the sweet chilli sauce, soy sauce, cornflour slurry and lime juice.

5. Heat until the sauce thickens. Then, add the fried chicken to the pan and toss to combine. Serve each portion with some rice and green beans and a garnish of spring onions and the thinly sliced chilli.

Popcorn Chicken

Low Carb High Protein

5 min prep + 15 min cook

This fakeaway recipe is surprisingly easy. It starts with a marinade that creates the juiciest, most tender chicken. These simple steps result in the tastiest bites, which dare I say, could even rival the Colonel's recipe.

Serves 5

250 g Greek yoghurt

2 tsp paprika

600 g boneless, skinless chicken breasts, cut into 2-cm chunks

200 g plain flour

3 tbsp cornflour

1 tsp onion powder

1 tsp garlic powder

4 tbsp rapeseed oil

tomato ketchup, BBQ sauce or mayonnaise, to serve

salt to taste

1. In a large bowl, add the Greek yoghurt with one teaspoon of the paprika and stir until combined. Add the diced chicken, stir until coated in the mix, then cover with clingfilm. Chill in the fridge for a minimum of one hour, but preferably 2–3 hours.

2. Next, stir together the flour, cornflour, the remaining paprika and the onion and garlic powders on a plate. Roll the marinated chicken pieces in the mix to coat and transfer to a parchment paper-lined baking sheet.

3. Preheat the oven to 100°C/80°C Fan.

4. Set a large, wide frying pan over a high heat and add one tablespoon of the rapeseed oil. Check if the oil is hot enough by placing a small piece of the chicken in the pan. If the chicken sizzles, you are ready to fry!

5. Fry the chicken in batches, ensuring the pieces are well-spaced and not touching (add more oil for each batch). Fry each batch for about four minutes in total, turning each piece after two minutes to ensure an even golden colour.

6. Remove from the pan and place on a plate lined with kitchen paper; immediately season with salt to taste. Keep the pieces warm in the oven until all the batches have been fried.

7. Serve with tomato ketchup, BBQ sauce or mayonnaise on the side for dipping!

Air Fryer

Follow steps 1-2. Preheat an air fryer to 200°C and grease the basket with a few sprays of oil. Add the chicken in three batches. Spray the battered chicken with a few sprays of oil before cooking for five minutes per batch, shaking halfway.

Homemade Fish & Chips

10 min prep + 15 min cook

It's the Number One, signature takeaway in the UK, so it only felt right to include it in my Fakeaways chapter. I was inspired to make this recipe when I realised how reasonably priced frozen white fish is in the supermarket. I don't usually request that you deep-fry any ingredient due to the cost of using a lot of oil, but I do here as the protein is relatively cheap, and the batter is made from cupboard staples (soda water is really cheap!). The result is the crispiest, fluffiest batter that you'll be amazed you made at home. If you usually hate mushy peas, I think these will be your gateway version - they're bright, creamy and delicious!

Serves 5

1 quantity Takeaway Chips (see page 210)

For the fish
700 g frozen white fish fillets, defrosted
90 g plain flour, plus extra for dusting
90 g cornflour
1 tsp baking powder
250 ml soda water
700 ml sunflower oil or vegetable oil, for frying
1 lemon, sliced into wedges to serve
salt to taste

For the 'mushy' peas
400 g frozen peas
50 g butter
small handful of fresh parsley, roughly chopped
salt to taste

1. Follow the method for Takeaway Chips on page 210.

2. Place the defrosted fish on a clean tea towel and pat dry. If the fish pieces are longer than those in the accompanying photo, cut them in half.

3. Meanwhile, to prepare the batter, add the plain flour, cornflour, baking powder and a pinch of salt to a bowl. Then add the soda water and whisk together. You should have a nice thick, smooth batter consistency.

4. Sprinkle some flour onto a plate, then dredge each of the fish pieces in flour to coat on both sides.

5. Meanwhile, set a deep pan over a high heat, add the oil and wait until it starts to bubble (test by adding a few drops of batter into the oil – it's hot enough when they sizzle).

6. Dunk a few pieces of fish into the batter mixture, then place the battered fish pieces carefully into the hot oil (2–3 pieces at one time, depending on the size of your fillets).

7. Deep-fry for around 1–2 minutes, before rotating with a long spatula so that each side fries evenly.

8. Remove from the pan with a slotted spoon (or two forks) allowing all the excess oil to drain back into the pot, then place on a wire rack. Season immediately with salt and repeat the process until all the fish pieces are cooked.

9. To prepare the peas, place them in a heatproof bowl with some water in the microwave and cook according to the packet instructions. Drain the peas and add the butter, chopped parsley and a large pinch of salt. Use a stick blender to blitz a few times to form a chunky consistency. You can blend a bit more if you want a really mushy texture.

10. Serve each portion of battered fish with some Takeaway Chips and mushy peas. Squeeze a wedge of lemon over the whole dish and tuck in!

Black Bean & Mushroom Burger

Freeze   Veggie

10 min prep + 23 min cook

To replicate a meaty burger, I thought the best combination would be black beans and mushrooms. I'm so pleased with the result, so much so that I would choose it over a meat burger at a BBQ. It's smoky, savoury and when paired with the melted Cheddar cheese, heaven. I like to serve mine with a side salad or Takeaway Chips (see page 210) or Grilled Sweetcorn with Tangy Mayo & Feta (see page 67).

Serves 6

250 g chestnut mushrooms, finely chopped
2 red onions, 1 diced and 1 thinly sliced
3 tbsp rapeseed oil
1 tsp ground cumin
3 garlic cloves, crushed
2 x 400 g cans black beans, drained and rinsed
120 g breadcrumbs
2 eggs
6 tbsp mayonnaise
1 tbsp hot sauce
6 Cheddar cheese slices
6 brioche buns
1 iceberg lettuce, shredded
salt and pepper to taste

If you don't want to serve all the burgers at once, you could make (but not cook) the patties and chill in the fridge for up to three days or freeze them for up to three months. When it's time to eat, let them defrost in the fridge overnight, using kitchen paper to remove any excess moisture before frying. Then follow step 5 onwards.

1. Set a non-stick frying pan over a low/medium heat, then add the mushrooms, diced red onion and one tablespoon of the oil. Season with salt and pepper and fry for around seven minutes, or until all the moisture is released and cooked off the mushrooms. For the final minute of frying time, add the cumin and garlic.

2. Meanwhile, put the black beans on a clean tea towel and pat to remove any excess moisture.

3. Allow the mushroom and onion mix to cool for two minutes, then add to a large bowl along with the black beans, breadcrumbs and eggs. Season with salt and pepper and combine.

4. Use a potato masher to roughly mash the black beans (not completely as otherwise the burgers will become too dense – some texture is good). Once roughly mashed, use your hands to form six burgers. Put the mayonnaise and hot sauce in a bowl and combine. Set aside for later.

5. Set the same non-stick frying pan over a medium heat and add one tablespoon of the rapeseed oil. Put three of the burgers in the pan and fry for four minutes on each side. When you rotate the burgers, add a slice of cheese to each and cover the pan with a lid, frying until the cheese has melted. Repeat for the remaining three burgers, adding the remaining rapeseed oil before frying.

6. Meanwhile, set a dry frying pan over a medium heat, split the brioche buns and toast, cut-side down, until lightly golden, about two minutes. You will have to toast the buns in batches as they won't all fit in one pan.

7. Assemble each toasted burger bun with a layer of the chilli mayo, some lettuce, a burger patty and some of the thinly sliced red onion. Top with a bun half (layered with more chilli mayo).

Fakeaways

Air-fried Crispy Cornflake Chicken Burger

10 min prep + 14 min cook

Note: *To make without an air fryer, add about 2 cm of rapeseed oil to a frying pan and shallow-fry the burgers over a medium/high heat for two minutes on each side. Transfer to a preheated 180°C/160°C Fan oven for 15–20 minutes until cooked through.*

This crusty, spicy, cornflake burger feels like it's straight out of a restaurant. The cornflake coating gives it that deep-fried feeling, which when air-fried with a tiny bit of oil, crisps up to form a heavenly batter. Using chicken thighs makes the most succulent burgers and it's one of my favourite recipes. Crushed up supermarket-brand cornflakes are a great budget alternative to breadcrumbs, as you get such a high volume for a fraction of the price!

Serves 6

650 g boneless, skinless chicken thighs
6 burger buns
6 tbsp mayonnaise
2 heads of baby gem lettuce, leaves separated
275 g shop-bought creamy coleslaw
4–6 jarred gherkins, drained and sliced
salt to taste

For the marinade
500 g natural yoghurt
1 tbsp chilli powder
1 tbsp smoked paprika
1 tsp onion powder
1 tsp garlic powder

For the cornflake crust
200 g cornflakes
½ tsp smoked paprika
1 tsp garlic powder
1 tsp onion powder
3 tbsp plain flour
2 eggs
oil spray
3 tbsp hot sauce, for drizzling

1. To make the marinade, add the yoghurt, chilli powder, smoked paprika and onion and garlic powders to a large bowl. Mix to combine and add the chicken thighs to the bowl. Stir to coat the chicken all over and cover with clingfilm. Pop in the fridge and leave to marinate for 2–4 hours.

2. Preheat the air fryer to 200°C for five minutes.

3. To make the cornflake crust, add the cornflakes to a bowl and roughly crush the flakes in your hand, creating varying sized pieces. Add the smoked paprika and the garlic and onion powders and mix to combine.

4. Put the flour on a plate. Add the eggs to a bowl and beat. Dredge the marinated chicken thighs in flour, then in egg, then into the cornflake mix, pressing the flakes into the chicken to ensure an even coating.

5. Spritz each piece of coated chicken with a few sprays of oil and place in the air fryer for seven minutes. Rotate and add a drizzle of hot sauce, then cook for another seven minutes.

6. Meanwhile, set a dry, non-stick frying pan over a medium heat, split the buns and toast in batches, cut-side down.

7. Once the chicken has cooked, remove from the air fryer and season immediately (and generously) with salt while still hot to help it stick.

8. Spread a layer of mayonnaise onto the buns, then add lettuce leaves, the chicken burgers, some creamy coleslaw and a few slices of gherkin. Top with the other bun halves and serve.

Fakeaways

Chicken Katsu Curry

Low Fat

High Protein

5 min prep + 30 min cook

Note: *If you're planning on dipping your chicken in breadcrumbs twice for an even crispier exterior, opt for double the amount of panko breadcrumbs when shopping (140 g).*

This Japanese-inspired curry is the ultimate fakeaway for a Friday night in. It might seem like a difficult dish to replicate, but this recipe is surprisingly easy and you can whip it up in less time than it takes for a takeaway to arrive. The fragrant sauce pairs perfectly with the crispy panko-crusted chicken breast. I can see why this is a favourite takeaway order and now one you can enjoy more frequently, for less cost.

Serves 6

For the sauce
1 tbsp rapeseed oil
2 onions, diced
1 carrot, thinly sliced
3 garlic cloves, crushed
1½ tbsp curry powder
1 tbsp peeled and grated fresh ginger
½ tsp ground turmeric
1 tbsp honey or brown sugar
1½ tbsp soy sauce
2 tbsp plain flour
600 ml chicken stock
salt and pepper to taste

For the chicken
3 boneless, skinless chicken breasts, about 650 g total weight
3 tbsp plain flour
2 eggs, lightly beaten
70–140 g panko breadcrumbs
2 tbsp rapeseed oil
300 g white or brown rice
spring onions, sliced, to garnish
pinch of chilli flakes, to garnish

1. Preheat the oven to 200°C/180°C Fan.

2. To make the sauce, set a deep, non-stick frying pan over a medium/low heat, add the rapeseed oil, onions and carrot and gently fry for about five minutes. Season with salt.

3. Add the garlic, curry powder, ginger, turmeric, honey or brown sugar, soy sauce and flour with a splash of the chicken stock. Gently fry for another minute before gradually pouring in the remaining chicken stock. Reduce to a simmer and allow to cook for 20 minutes.

4. Meanwhile, prepare the chicken. Hold each chicken breast flat with the palm of your hand on a chopping board and use a sharp knife to slice horizontally from the thickest part of the breast all the way through, to create two equal-sized pieces. Start the crispy chicken conveyor belt by rolling each piece in flour, then dip in the beaten egg and finally coat in the breadcrumbs. For even crispier chicken, re-dip into the egg and then the breadcrumbs.

5. Drizzle one tablespoon of the rapeseed oil onto a large baking sheet and lay out the breadcrumbed chicken. Drizzle over the remaining rapeseed oil and pop in the oven for 12 minutes. Remove the baking sheet, rotate the chicken pieces carefully and return to the oven to cook for a further 12 minutes.

6. Meanwhile, cook the rice according to the packet instructions.

7. Take the thickened sauce, pour into a blender and blitz. Reheat before serving if necessary.

8. Slice the chicken diagonally and serve each portion with some rice, a ladle of the sauce and garnish with the spring onions and chilli flakes.

Tofu Banh Mi

10 min prep + 8 min cook

A Banh Mi is a Vietnamese sandwich that traditionally involves a crusty bread roll, pâté, mayonnaise, crunchy veggies and some sort of meat – usually pork. This is my simplified vegetarian take – by coating tofu pieces in cornflour and frying with soy sauce and honey, you get a crispy, umami-packed, meaty-textured substitute for pork that is so flavourful. I've served this to many friends who hate tofu and they were surprised how much they liked it. You can whip this up as a speedy lunch and pack in your bag to take on the go. Fresh and delicious.

Serves 4

400 g extra firm tofu
3 tbsp rice vinegar
1 tbsp sugar
1 tsp salt
200 ml water
2 carrots, cut into thin batons
3 tbsp cornflour
2 tbsp rapeseed oil
3 tbsp soy sauce
1 tbsp honey
1 large baguette (400 g), cut into
  4 equal-sized pieces
4 tbsp mayonnaise
1 cucumber, sliced in half
  lengthways, then diagonally
  into thin pieces
handful of fresh coriander,
  roughly torn
4–8 tsp sriracha or hot sauce,
  for drizzling
2 mild red chillies, thinly sliced

1. Start by draining the tofu. Place it in a clean tea towel, fold up the sides and squeeze the tofu to remove any excess liquid. Cut the tofu into thin planks, around 3½ cm x 8 cm and pat each plank dry with some kitchen paper.

2. Meanwhile, to a large jar, add the rice vinegar, sugar, salt and 150 millilitres of the water. Add the carrot batons and leave to soak while you prepare all the other sandwich components.

3. Pour the cornflour onto a large plate, spreading it out. Dredge the tofu planks in the cornflour, coating all over and shaking off any excess.

4. Meanwhile, set a large, non-stick frying pan over a high heat and add the rapeseed oil. Once hot, add the tofu planks. Reduce the heat to medium and fry for about four minutes on one side. When the tofu has become rigid and golden on the underside, then add the remaining 50 millilitres of water to the bottom of the pan, along with the soy sauce and honey. Turn the tofu planks over to cook for a further 3–4 minutes, ensuring that the tofu is fully coated in the sauce.

5. Slice each portion of baguette in half lengthways and press the soft insides of the bread towards the crust to allow more room for the filling. Spread over a layer of mayonnaise, add some crispy soy tofu pieces, cucumber, pickled carrots and some coriander. Drizzle over the sriracha, add some slices of chilli, then squash the baguette closed and dig in!

Prawn Firecracker Curry

5 min prep + 15 min cook

This is a spice lovers' ultimate fakeaway experience, which happens to come together in around 20 minutes for a fraction of the price of a takeaway. Depending on your budget, you can increase or decrease the serving of prawns to make quantities cost effective - be sure to buy frozen prawns to keep within budget. This recipe is a simplified version of the classic as I use sweet chilli sauce and fresh chillies, which are widely available, instead of more expensive oyster sauce, sriracha and fish sauce. I'd stay in on a Friday for this one - it's that good!

Serves 5

375 g white rice
2 tbsp rapeseed oil
30 g peeled and chopped fresh ginger
50 g spring onions, finely chopped
3 chillies, finely chopped
3 garlic cloves, finely chopped
600 ml fish stock
2 tbsp soy sauce
4 tbsp sweet chilli sauce
500 g frozen mixed peppers, defrosted
160 g mangetout
1 tbsp cornflour, plus 2 tbsp water mixed to form the cornflour slurry)
200–400 g frozen peeled, raw large prawns, defrosted
salt and pepper to taste
5 lime wedges, to garnish
small pinch of chilli flakes per serving (optional)
small pinch of chilli powder per serving (optional)

1. Cook the rice in a large pan of boiling water according to the packet instructions (mine cooked in 12 minutes). Drain and set aside.

2. Meanwhile, set a non-stick frying pan over a medium heat and add the rapeseed oil, ginger, spring onions and chillies, frying for three minutes. Season with salt and pepper.

3. Add the garlic and fry for a further two minutes before adding the stock, soy sauce and sweet chilli sauce.

4. Squeeze all the moisture out of the defrosted peppers before adding to the pan with the mangetout. Cover with a lid and simmer for around four minutes.

5. Remove the lid, add the cornflour slurry and prawns and stir to combine, ensuring that all the prawns are submerged. Cover with the lid and cook for three minutes.

6. Add some cooked rice to a small bowl and press until firm, flip upside down and turn out the rice onto the middle of a plate. Repeat for all servings. Serve some of the curry around the rice and garnish each portion with a lime wedge and a light sprinkle of chilli flakes and chilli powder, if you like.

Add all of the ingredients used in steps 2-4. Cook for two hours on high or three hours on low. Then, when it's time to eat, add the prawns and cornflour slurry and cook for 20 minutes on high.

Slow Cooker Butter Chicken Curry

5 min prep + 1-3 hr cook

This recipe is warming and comforting, perfect for a night in. You can pop all the ingredients in the slow cooker and let it work its magic. I love making this ahead of a movie night with friends as you can host without having to miss any gossip. I've simplified the spices in comparison to a takeaway so that you can grab the ingredients from your cupboard and save money. The result is a fragrant, delicious curry that requires little-to-no effort. Oh, and you can meal prep it, too.

Serves 6

- 900 g boneless, skinless chicken thighs
- 1 onion, finely diced
- 75 g butter, cut into cubes
- 2 tbsp peeled and finely grated fresh ginger
- 4 garlic cloves, crushed
- 2 x 500 g cartons passata
- 2 tsp ground cumin
- 2 tsp garam masala
- ½ tsp ground turmeric
- 1 tsp sugar
- 1 chicken stock cube
- 450 g white rice
- 1 large head of broccoli, cut into florets
- 100 ml single cream
- juice of ½ lime
- small handful of fresh coriander, roughly chopped to serve
- salt and pepper to taste

1. Add the chicken thighs, onion, butter, ginger, garlic, passata, spices, sugar and crumbled chicken stock cube into the slow cooker. Season with salt and pepper. Stir to combine everything and pop the lid on the slow cooker. Cook for 1–2 hours on high or for 2–3 hours on low. Slice a piece of chicken after the lower amount of time to check that it is cooked through, although you don't want to risk drying out the chicken either.

2. Twenty minutes before you are ready to eat, cook the rice according to the packet instructions and steam the broccoli florets for six minutes.

3. When the slow cooker timer goes off, stir the cream and lime juice into the curry. Remove the pieces of chicken, slice into bite-sized pieces and add them back into the slow cooker, stirring them through.

4. Serve each portion of curry with a portion of rice and broccoli and top with coriander.

To make without a slow cooker:

1. To a large saucepan, add the onion, ginger and butter. Season with salt and fry over a medium heat for 5 minutes. Then add the spices, sugar and garlic to fry for a further minute before adding the passata, chicken thighs, chicken stock, and a pinch of salt and pepper. Cook for 25 minutes over a low/medium heat, then stir in the cream and lime juice before serving with rice and broccoli. Top with fresh coriander.

Divide portions of curry, rice and broccoli between meal prep containers. Seal and chill in the fridge for up to three days or freeze for up to three months. Be sure to chill the rice and curry as soon as it is cool - don't leave the rice at room temperature for long. Defrost frozen portions in the fridge overnight. To reheat, microwave on high for two minutes, then top with freshly chopped coriander.

Peri-Peri Chicken Thighs

5 min prep + 23-28 min cook, plus 1 hr marinating

These Portuguese-inspired chicken thighs are spicy, smoky, tender and so, so delicious - my favourite recipe when I want to get my grill on. I love bird's eye chillies as they are the cheapest to buy in the supermarket, but give maximum heat. If you want a milder spice, opt for mild chillies (chunkier-looking ones) and remove the seeds - these are also really reasonably priced. You can either meal prep this recipe to enjoy with salads, veg and rice or pair with my Takeaway Chips (see page 210) for a Friday night treat.

Serves 5-6

200 g jarred roasted red
  peppers, plus 1 tbsp brine
1 tsp honey
5 garlic cloves, smashed
4-6 bird's eye chillies (stems
  removed), roughly chopped
2 tsp smoked paprika
1 tsp dried oregano
900 g boneless, skinless chicken
  thighs
2 tbsp rapeseed oil
chopped fresh parsley leaves,
  to serve (optional)
salt and pepper to taste

1. Start by adding the roasted peppers, one tablespoon of their brine, the honey, smashed garlic, chillies, smoked paprika, oregano and salt and pepper to a food processor. Blitz to form a smooth marinade. If you have a blender rather than a food processor, you might need to chop the garlic and chillies a little bit more before adding them to the blender.

2. Pour the spicy peri-peri marinade into a large bowl, add the chicken thighs and mix together until the meat is well coated. Cover with clingfilm and chill in the fridge for a minimum of one hour. If possible, marinate for 5-12 hours.

3. Preheat the oven to 220°C/200°C Fan.

4. Set a griddle pan over a high heat, add one tablespoon of the rapeseed oil and sear half of the chicken thighs on one side for around four minutes until char lines appear. Remove and place on a baking tray, seared-side up. Repeat with the other half of the chicken thighs, adding the remaining rapeseed oil and searing the chicken on one side. Once all the thighs are seared and on the baking tray, brush over any leftover marinade and season with an extra pinch of salt.

5. Cook in the oven for 15 minutes. Depending on the size of the chicken thighs, you may need to cook for a further five minutes (slice the largest piece in half to check). Top with parsley, if you like, and dig in!

These chicken thighs can be enjoyed hot or cold - they make for a vibrant, spicy protein in a salad (one of my fave ways to enjoy them). Or reheat in the microwave on high for two minutes as part of a hot dish. Store in the fridge in sealed containers for up to three days or freeze for up to two months. Defrost overnight in the fridge.

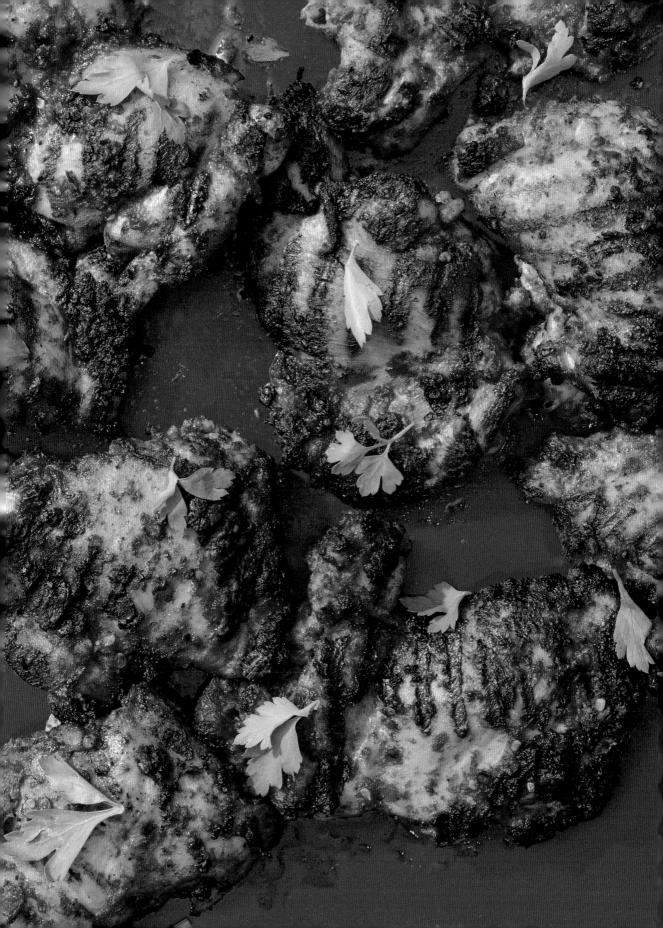

Smoky Pork Tacos

High Protein

5 min prep + 13 min cook

One of the most popular taco dishes is Pork Carnitas. They are made using pork shoulder that is deeply spiced and shredded. Unfortunately, pork shoulder is pricey and you need to use a lot of energy to cook it. Enter pork mince! With the seasoning and spices, plus the way that the mince is cooked in this recipe, it acts as an amazing substitute. Smoky and mildly hot (you can skip the chilli flakes if you wanna turn down the heat), the pork contrasts amazingly with the vibrant crunchy cabbage and the tangy coriander sauce. Plus, it takes under 20 minutes to make.

Serves 5

10 tortilla wraps

For the pickled cabbage
1 red cabbage, thinly sliced
juice of ½ lime
1 tsp sugar
½ tsp salt

For the spiced pork
1 tbsp rapeseed oil
1 onion, cut into thin wedges
1 tsp chilli flakes, plus a pinch
   (optional), to garnish
500 g pork mince
2 tbsp tomato purée
3 garlic cloves, crushed
1 tsp ground coriander
2 tsp paprika
1 tsp ground cumin
salt and pepper to taste

For the sauce
large handful of fresh coriander,
   roughly chopped, plus extra to
   garnish
300 ml soured cream
juice of ½ lime
pinch of salt

1. To make the pickled red cabbage, add the cabbage to a bowl with the lime juice, sugar and salt. Mix to combine, then set aside to 'quick pickle'.

2. Next, make the spiced pork. Set a non-stick frying pan over a medium heat and add the rapeseed oil and onion wedges. Season with salt and pepper and a teaspoon of chilli flakes. Fry for about five minutes.

3. After the five minutes cooking time, move the onions to the outside of the pan and add the pork mince. Leave the mince to brown (breaking it apart with a spatula, but not stirring) for about four minutes. Next, add the tomato purée, garlic and spices. Season with salt and pepper and fry for a further four minutes, stirring frequently.

4. Meanwhile, make the sauce. Add the coriander, soured cream, lime juice and a pinch of salt to a food processor or blender and blitz.

5. Assemble the tortilla wraps/tacos with a layer of the pickled cabbage, some spiced pork mince and a drizzle of the tangy coriander sauce. Garnish with some chopped coriander and optional extra chilli flakes to finish. Fold and enjoy!

Meal Prep

Make all the elements as detailed in the method and store in separate sealed containers in the fridge for up to three days. The spiced pork mince can also be frozen. When it's time to eat, defrost, then reheat a serving of pork in the microwave on high.Assemble and enjoy.

Sheet Pan Pizza – Three Ways

Freeze

5 min prep + 23–28 min cook

I've replicated what I believe to be the three most popular pizza flavours and I love the results. Choose your favourite topping to spread across one pizza, or if you can't come to an agreement with those you're sharing with, mix and match the toppings on each quarter. Ready-rolled pizza dough is such a great cheat ingredient – it's cheap, reduces mess and one large pizza shared between four reduces energy usage and oven space. If using your own toppings, ensure that any uncooked veggies are thinly sliced so they cook in the short amount of oven time.

Serves 4

For the base
400 g (1 pack) ready-rolled pizza
  dough
100 ml passata
1 tsp dried oregano
250 g (2 balls) mozzarella,
  drained and torn into pieces
handful of fresh basil leaves,
  to serve
salt and pepper to taste

Pizza 1 – La Reine toppings
handful of mushrooms, thinly
  sliced
100 g wafer thin ham, roughly
  torn
small handful of pitted black
  olives, sliced
salt and pepper to taste

Pizza 2 – Veggie Supreme toppings
½ red pepper, seeded and thinly
  sliced
½ orange pepper, seeded and
  thinly sliced
½ red onion, thinly sliced
100 g cherry tomatoes, halved
salt and pepper to taste

1. Preheat the oven to 180°C/160°C Fan.

2. For the pizza base, line a flat baking sheet with parchment paper and unroll the dough onto it. Cook in the middle of the oven for eight minutes.

3. Meanwhile, add the passata and oregano to a bowl with some salt and pepper to season and mix.

4. Remove the pizza base from the oven and allow it to deflate before spreading over the passata mixture.

5. Blot the torn mozzarella with some kitchen paper to remove excess moisture. Scatter the cheese over the pizza and then add the toppings of your choice. Pop back in the oven for 15–20 minutes, or until the base is firm and the cheese is golden and crispy.

6. Top with basil leaves, garnish with chilli flakes for the Sloppy Giuseppe and season with salt and pepper before serving.

Pizza 3 – Sloppy Giuseppe
  toppings
1 green pepper, seeded and
  thinly sliced
500 g beef mince, browned in a
  pan with ground spices, black
  pepper and oil for 8 minutes
2 tsp chilli powder
1 tsp rapeseed oil
salt and pepper to taste
1 tsp chilli flakes, to garnish

Takeaway Chips

Gluten Free Vegan

5 min prep + 35–40 min cook, plus 30 min soaking

I knew that including a chip recipe would be a necessity in this book – good chips are the delicious support act to so many dishes. With this method, you get the crispiest chips without having to deep-fry the potatoes. It's all about removing the excess starch, ensuring they have enough space on the baking sheet to crisp up and roasting at a high temperature. You can pair this with my Peri-Peri Chicken Thighs (see page 204) for the ultimate chicken takeaway experience, pair with any burger in the book (head to page 192 or page 194) or enjoy with your favourite sauces as a movie snack. If you want to replicate the chippy vibe, add a light drizzle of malt vinegar.

Serves 5

1.2 kg potatoes, approx. 10–12 cm in length
1 tsp garlic powder
6 tbsp rapeseed oil or any vegetable oil
1 tsp salt
pepper to taste (optional)

1. Slice the potatoes into thin chips, with an approximate width of 1½ cm. I left the skin on as I love the flavour, texture and less prep. You can peel them first, if you prefer.

2. Place them in a bowl of cold water, this will remove any excess starch and maximise crispiness. Set aside for 30 minutes.

3. Preheat the oven to 220°C/200°C Fan.

4. Drain the chips, place them on a clean tea towel and pat dry. Once dry, add them back into a dry bowl along with the garlic powder, four tablespoons of the rapeseed oil and the salt. Mix together to ensure the chips are evenly coated.

5. Line two baking sheets with foil and coat the foil with the remaining rapeseed oil (one tablespoon per sheet to prevent sticking). Add half of the chips to each sheet and distribute evenly so the pieces are not overlapping or touching.

6. Place both sheets in the oven to cook for 20 minutes, before rotating the chips and swapping their placement in the oven. Cook for a further 15–20 minutes until golden and crispy.

Air Fryer

Preheat the air fryer to 195°C. Follow the same method, but air fry the chips in two batches, adding the extra tablespoon of rapeseed oil into the air fryer basket with each batch. Fry for ten minutes, then shake the basket and fry for another 15 minutes.

Fakeaways

Sweet

Peanut Butter Rice Crispy Treats

Freeze   **Veggie**

10 min prep

This recipe is a mix of standard cupboard ingredients – a bar of chocolate, a jar of peanut butter, a jar of honey and a box of rice snaps cereal is all you need to make the easiest sweet treat. I love a dessert where no cooking is needed – these crisp bites only require a microwave and space in your fridge. The salty peanut butter has the ideal amount of savoury to balance out the sweetness of the chocolate layer. These more-ish squares are also freezable if you want to prevent yourself from eating the whole batch in a few days.

Makes 12

150 g smooth peanut butter
6 tbsp honey
100 g rice snaps cereal
200 g milk or plain chocolate

1. Line a rectangular dish with some clingfilm. I used a 25 cm x 18 cm glass dish, or for thicker slices, use a smaller 20 cm x 15 cm dish.

2. Take a large microwavable bowl and add the peanut butter and honey. Place in the microwave on a medium heat for 15 seconds to loosen the mix up and then stir to combine.

3. Add the rice snaps to the bowl and stir until they are coated in the peanut butter and honey mix.

4. Pour the mix into the lined dish and spread out evenly. Make sure the rice snaps are packed in tightly, pressing down firmly using a solid object (I used a glass measuring jug).

5. Put a heatproof bowl over a pan of simmering water (not touching the water), break up the chocolate into the bowl and stir occasionally until melted. Pour the melted chocolate into the dish, over the rice snaps, and spread out evenly using a spatula.

6. Chill in the fridge for a couple of hours, or if you are in a rush, place in the freezer for one hour instead. To remove from the dish, pull the clingfilm gently to transfer from the dish to a chopping board. Slice into squares with a sharp knife and try not to finish the whole lot in one sitting.

Apple Pie Pastry

Freeze   Veggie

10 min prep + 20 min cook

If you've ever wanted to make the most popular dessert from everyone's favourite Fast Food restaurant, look no further. These are easy to make and you can whip them up for a fraction of the price. Better yet, they can be frozen! I like to double the batch and freeze half, so that you can grab a serving and throw it straight into the oven for the perfect, low-hassle sweet treat. I use Cox apples because of their slightly sharp flavour, but Braeburns or Pink Lady varieties would also be good.

Makes 5

25 g butter
1 tbsp caster sugar, plus extra
  for sprinkling
pinch of ground cinnamon
2 Cox apples, peeled, cored and
  chopped into small cubes
½ tsp cornflour
375 g (1 pack) ready-rolled puff
  pastry sheet

1. Preheat the oven to 200°C/180°C Fan.

2. Set a pan over a medium heat and add the butter, sugar, cinnamon and the apples. Cover with a lid and cook for 4–5 minutes until the apples are just tender, stirring them occasionally.

3. Sprinkle over the cornflour and stir. Tip the apples out of the pan onto a plate and allow to cool for ten minutes, then place in the freezer for a further ten minutes until the apples are cold – don't allow them to freeze.

4. Remove the pastry from the fridge ten minutes before using. Unroll directly onto a baking sheet using the parchment paper that the pastry comes with to line the sheet. Lay the pastry horizontally in front of you. Use a sharp knife to cut vertically into five equal strips. Place a large spoonful of apple on the top half of each strip. Dampen the edges of the pastry with cold water, then fold the lower part of the pastry strip over the apple filling to meet the top of the pastry strip. Seal the edges by pressing together with the tines of a fork.

5. Brush the tops very lightly with cold water and sprinkle with sugar.

6. Bake in the oven for 15 minutes until risen and golden brown, then serve warm, sprinkled with a little more sugar, if you like.

Loaded Speculoos Banana Split

5 min prep

Note: *Want to elevate this dish even further? Why not serve it with my No-churn Salted Caramel Ice Cream (see page 222).*

This should be your go-to dessert when you want to whip something up instantly, without compromising on indulgence and sweetness. It takes five minutes to make and the only fresh ingredient you need on hand is a banana – the rest is hopefully in your cupboard or freezer. Feel free to customise with your favourite toppings.

Serves 1

- 1 tbsp speculoos spread (I use Lotus Biscoff Spread)
- 2–3 tbsp boiling water
- 1 banana, peeled and halved lengthways
- 2 scoops (120 ml) vanilla ice cream
- 1 digestive biscuit, or biscuit of choice

1. Add the speculoos spread and boiling water to a bowl and mix to loosen into a drizzling sauce.

2. Place the banana into an oval serving dish and scoop the ice cream in the middle of the banana halves.

3. Crumble the digestive biscuit over the banana and ice cream, then drizzle over the speculoos sauce and tuck in!

Carrot Cake Cheesecake

Veggie

20 min prep + 20 min cook, plus setting time

This is a pretty self-centred choice of flavour combination as I've chosen my two favourite desserts and combined them into one – but I'm so glad I did! The result is a crowd-pleaser for cheesecake and carrot cake lovers everywhere. So simple and quick to make, and it keeps in the fridge for 3–4 days if you can resist it for that long!

Serves 12

For the cake
50 ml vegetable oil
2 large eggs
100 g light soft brown sugar
1 tsp ground mixed spice or ground cinnamon
75 g carrots, coarsely grated
75 g walnut pieces, chopped
100 g self-raising flour

For the topping
600 g (2 packs) full-fat cream cheese
1 orange
6 tbsp icing sugar
300 ml double cream
3 tbsp water
2 tbsp caster sugar (for the peel)

1. Preheat the oven to 180°C/160°C Fan. Line the base and sides of a 20 cm round, springform cake tin with parchment paper.

2. To make the cake, place the oil, eggs, brown sugar and mixed spice into a large bowl and whisk for a minute, then add the carrots, walnuts (saving a few to decorate the top of the cake later) and flour and stir until combined.

3. Pour into the prepared cake tin, spread the surface out evenly and bake for 20 minutes until just firm in the centre. Remove from the oven and allow to cool in the tin.

4. To make the topping, put the cream cheese into a large bowl and add the finely grated zest of half the orange, the icing sugar and cream. Use an electric hand whisk to beat until really thick, then spread on top of the cold carrot cake. Refrigerate for at least one hour until set. Remove from the tin to serve.

5. Meanwhile, to make the orange strands, peel the remaining orange half with a vegetable peeler, shaving off long matchsticks. Set a small pan over a medium heat and add the peel, water and one tablespoon of the caster sugar, then boil for 2–3 minutes.

6. Drain in a sieve and pat the peel dry with kitchen paper, then toss the peel in the remaining caster sugar. Leave to dry and arrange on top of the chilled cheesecake just before serving. Add the reserved walnuts to decorate.

No-churn Salted Caramel Ice Cream

Freeze Gluten Free Veggie

10 min prep + 4 hr freeze

This is so good – you'll never bother buying ice cream again when you discover how delicious and easy it is to make! You don't even need an ice-cream machine. Although I love this recipe just as it is, you could easily customise it with dark chocolate, chopped pretzels... Use your imagination. I'm so excited for you to try this one!

Serves 10

397 g dulce de leche (I use 1 x 397 g can Carnation Caramel)
600 ml whipping cream
1 tsp sea salt

1. Reserve four tablespoons of the dulce de leche for later, and pour the remaining caramel into a bowl. Beat lightly to loosen, then add the cream and whip with an electric hand whisk until smooth and thick. Stir in the salt and pour into a freezer-proof container.

2. Drizzle the reserved dulce de leche on top and gently swirl it through the mixture with a knife. Smooth the top, then cover and freeze for at least four hours.

3. Remove from the freezer 20 minutes before serving.

Hazelnut Spread Swirled Banana Bread

Freeze   **Veggie**

15 min prep + 1 hr 30 min cook

Just look at those swirls! This is such a fun, delicious recipe that makes you feel like an artist – stirring chocolate hazelnut spread into a moist banana bread mixture adds a nutty, rich twist that elevates this much-loved bake. It's a great one to make ahead and slice into individual servings. Freeze in portions and pop into a non-stick pan to reheat when you're ready to eat! Sooo tasty.

Serves 14

150 g butter or margarine at room temperature, plus extra for greasing
350 g self-raising flour
350 g caster sugar
3 large eggs, beaten
3 ripe bananas (225 g peeled weight), peeled and mashed
200 g chocolate hazelnut spread, plus (optional) extra for drizzling

1. Preheat the oven to 180°C/160°C Fan. Grease and line a 900 g loaf tin with parchment paper.

2. Place the butter in a bowl with the flour and rub together with your fingers until it resembles breadcrumbs. Add the sugar, eggs and bananas and mix until combined.

3. Remove about one-third of the mixture into another bowl and stir in the chocolate hazelnut spread until combined.

4. Layer one-third of the pale mixture into the base of the tin, spreading out right up to the edge. Next, add some of the chocolate mixture to the centre and then spread alternate layers of each until you've used all the mixture up. Gravity will work its magic and form the swirls that you see in the photo.

5. Bake for 1 hour and 30 minutes until a skewer or cocktail stick comes out clean when inserted into the centre. Remove from the oven and allow to cool in the tin for ten minutes. Turn out onto a wire rack and allow to cool fully. Drizzle over a little extra chocolate hazelnut spread to decorate, if you like, before serving.

Oat Biscuit
Berry Crumble

5 min prep + 20-25 min cook

Why bother making a crumble topping when you can just crush a packet of biscuits and sprinkle them over some frozen fruit to make the perfect comforting pud? Frozen mixed berries are so inexpensive and you don't have to think about when to use them by as they're frozen at peak freshness. I love the variety and flavour you get in the mixed berry bags - choose your favourite summer fruits, blackberries, blueberries, whatever combo you like! With only four ingredients, it couldn't be easier to create such a crowd-pleasing dessert. Feel free to double the batch (as I have in the photo) to serve to a larger group.

Serves 4

500 g frozen mixed berries
1 tsp cornflour
2 tbsp cold water or orange juice
300 g sweet oat-based
  supermarket-brand biscuits
custard or cream, to serve

1. Preheat the oven to 180°C/160°C Fan.

2. Spread the frozen berries into a shallow, ovenproof dish, sprinkle with the cornflour, stir well, then pour over the cold water or orange juice. Bake in the oven for ten minutes.

3. Place the biscuits in a sandwich bag and bash with a rolling pin into a rubble with some coarse chunks. Remove the dish from the oven, sprinkle the crumble over the fruit and return to the oven for a further 10–15 minutes until golden and the fruit has softened. Serve with custard, cream or on its own!

Chocolate Soufflés

Gluten Free · **Veggie**

15 min prep + 12–15 min cook

These are so incredibly easy to make, so delicious to eat and they only have five ingredients. The soufflés have to be made at the last minute and you should serve them straight from the oven to wow your crowd with their amazing inflated centres. Although already super-chocolatey, I have taken it a step further and topped these with chocolate sauce. You could also drizzle over any leftover cream that you might have from the recipe itself.

Makes 6 small or 4 large

For the soufflés
1 tbsp butter, for greasing
5 tbsp caster sugar
170 g dark chocolate (60% cocoa solids), grated
2 tbsp double cream
5 eggs, separated

For the sauce
25 g butter
1 tbsp caster sugar
30 g dark chocolate (60% cocoa solids), chopped

1. Preheat the oven to 200°C/180°C Fan.

2. Rub the inside of four 200-millilitre or six 150-millilitre soufflé dishes or ramekins with the butter, then sprinkle the insides with one tablespoon of the caster sugar, rolling the dishes so the sugar coats the bottom and sides.

3. To make the soufflés, add the chocolate and cream to a heatproof bowl set over a pan of simmering water (but not touching the water). Heat until melted, stirring occasionally (or microwave in 30-second bursts, stirring to ensure the chocolate doesn't burn). Remove from the heat and cool a little.

4. Whisk the egg whites in a clean, grease-free bowl with an electric hand whisk until they form stiff peaks, then add the remaining four tablespoons of sugar, one teaspoon at a time, whisking until smooth and glossy.

5. Stir one egg yolk into the melted chocolate and cream mixture until smooth, then stir in the remaining egg yolks.

6. Add one heaped spoonful of meringue to the chocolate, folding in until just smooth, then fold all the chocolate mixture into the meringue until evenly mixed. Mix until the meringue and chocolate are just combined – if you overmix, your soufflés won't rise. Divide the mixture between the prepared dishes or ramekins, wiping the edges if necessary.

7. Place the dishes in the oven, reduce the heat to 180°C/160°C Fan and bake for 12–15 minutes until they feel just firm to the touch but have a wobble in the centre. The longer you cook them the firmer they will be – if you like them gooey inside, cook for 12 minutes, but no longer than 15 minutes or they will be more like cakes.

8. While the soufflés are baking, make the sauce. Set a small pan over a medium heat and add the butter and sugar, allowing them to melt. Add the chocolate and cook for one minute until smooth. Set aside and then spoon over the chocolate soufflés as soon as they come out of the oven, before they have time to sink. Dig in!

Meal Planners & Shopping Lists

As mentioned in the beginning of the book, I plan out multiple meals within a week ensuring that there's a balance of cross-over ingredients to keep the costs down and write up shopping lists to make sure I don't stray from the plan when I'm in the supermarket.

The five meal plans in this section put these methods into practice to help you save time, money and help take the stress out of planning. Usually, I prep three recipes as I'm often just cooking for me, but I've increased these plans to five that feed five or six people, so that they accommodate families too. Each of these plans should cost around £25 per week and all of the ingredients are listed for each plan. Lots of the recipes can be enjoyed as lunch or dinner so you can mix them up depending on what you're craving. Some of the recipes are freezable so that you can implement the freezer cycle mentioned earlier in the book (see page 9). My hope is that you can build on these lists and create your own as you find your favourites!

Meal Plan 1

- - - - - - - - - - - - - - - - -

**Creamy Sun-dried
Tomato & Pork Risotto**
Page 146

Harissa Yoghurt Orzo
Page 88

**Spiced Chicken Drumsticks
with Roasted Veg & Couscous**
Page 110

**Spinach & Artichoke
Stuffed Courgette Boats**
Page 116

**Goats' Cheese, Spinach
& Basil Linguine**
Page 160

Further Cost Savings
Buy a larger pot of crème
fraîche (around 300 ml) and
use in place of the yoghurt
for recipes 2 and 3. Loosen
with a little water to replicate
yoghurt. Check the frozen
section for potential
savings on meat.

Shared Ingredients
Sun-dried tomatoes,
garlic, frozen spinach,
lemon, Greek yoghurt
and parsley

Fresh
3 onions
9 courgettes
1 bulb of garlic
Fresh basil
2 lemons
Fresh parsley
1 red pepper
1 aubergine

Dairy
150 ml crème fraîche
150 g Greek yoghurt
400 g cream cheese (2 packs)
250 g mozzarella (2 balls)
125 g goats' cheese

Meat & Seafood
500 g pork mince
1 kg chicken drumsticks

Pantry
170 g sun-dried tomatoes
375 g risotto rice
4 tbsp tomato purée
400 g can chickpeas
500 g couscous
500 g orzo
90 g artichokes (jar)
500 g linguine
4 tbsp hariss

Cupboard Essentials
1 tbsp extra virgin olive oil
Salt and pepper
2 tsp smoked paprika
1 tsp ground cumin
1 tsp ground cinnamon
6 tbsp olive oil
Chilli flakes
4 chicken stock cubes

Frozen
560 g frozen spinach

Meal Plan 2

- - - - - - - - - - - - - - -

Red Cashew Curry
Page 152

**Ginger & Lime Chicken
Legs with Coconut Rice**
Page 142

**Chopped Mango Salad with
a Creamy Basil Dressing**
Page 50

Mushroom Rigatoni Ragù
Page 82

Smoky Pork Tacos
Page 206

Further Cost Savings
Purchase frozen broccoli to
use across recipes 1 and 2.
Check the frozen section for
potential savings on meat.

Fresh
2 onions
2 garlic bulbs
Fresh basil
3 limes
1 mango
2 red chillies
1 aubergine
1 head broccoli
250 g cherry tomatoes
1 cucumber
60 g rocket
50 g spring onions
100 g Tenderstem broccoli
250 g chestnut mushrooms
Fresh coriander
2 red cabbages
4 tbsp fresh ginger
1 red onion

Dairy
300 ml soured cream

Meat & Seafood
1.1 kg chicken legs
500 g pork mince

Pantry
1 tube tomato purée
2 vegetable stock cubes
2 x 400 g cans coconut milk
200 g red lentils
150 g cashews
600 g white rice
2 chicken stock cubes
400 g rigatoni
35 g panko breadcrumbs
180 g tortilla chips
10 tortilla wraps

Cupboard Essentials
4 tbsp olive oil
1½ tbsp curry powder
Salt and pepper
1 tbsp rapeseed oil
Extra virgin olive oil
1 tsp sugar
Flaky salt
1 tsp chilli flakes
1 tsp ground coriander
2 tsp paprika
1 tsp ground cumin

Frozen
300 g frozen peppers

**Shared
Ingredients**
Garlic, ginger, tomato
purée, cashews, rice,
lime, basil, coriander

Meal Plan 3

- - - - - - - - - - - - -

**Tortilla-crusted
Chicken Caesar Salad**
Page 48

Rigatoni alla Carbonara
Page 85

**Saag Paneer with
Rice & Naan**
Page 104

**Tuna Rice Bowl with
Crispy Cavolo Nero**
Page 170

Tofu Banh Mi
Page 198

Further Cost Savings
Use hard cheese
interchangeably with
Parmesan. Substitute cavolo
nero with kale if you prefer.
Check the frozen section for
potential savings on meat.

**Shared
Ingredients**
Garlic, eggs,
Parmesan, rice, ginger,
sriracha, coriander

Fresh
2 lemons
2 limes
1 bulb of garlic
1 onion
2 carrots
1½ tbsp fresh ginger
150 g cavolo nero
Fresh coriander
50 g spring onion
1 cucumber
2 mild red chillies
400 g extra firm tofu
2 heads of little gem lettuce

Dairy
8 eggs
110 g Parmesan
4 tbsp natural yoghurt
225 g (1 block) paneer

Meat & Seafood
350 g (2) chicken breasts
160 g pancetta

Pantry
11 tbsp mayonnaise
120 g tortilla chips
400 g rigatoni
500 g white rice
4 mini naans
4 x 145 g cans tuna in brine
5 tbsp sriracha
5 tbsp soy sauce
1 large baguette (400g)

Cupboard Essentials
4 tbsp rapeseed oil
2 tbsp plain flour
Salt and pepper
2 tbsp olive oil
2 tsp garam masala
1 vegetable stock cube
3 tbsp rice vinegar
1 tbsp sugar
3 tbsp cornflour
2 tbsp rapeseed oil
1 tbsp honey
1 tbsp Dijon mustard

Frozen
250 g frozen spinach

Meal Plan 4

- - - - - - - - - - - - - - -

Aubergine Parmigiana
Page 120

Slow Cooker Chicken with Nduja Brothy Beans
Page 38

Chicken Tzatziki Bowl
Page 58

Stove-top Mushroom Lasagne
Page 138

Nduja Sausage & Mascarpone Pasta
Page 132

Further Cost Savings
Whichever onion you prefer out of white/red, choose a bag of 4–5 onions to save money. Use hard cheese interchangeably with Parmesan. Share the fresh thyme between the brothy beans and pasta, in place of fresh rosemary for the beans. Check the frozen section for any savings on meat.

Shared Ingredients
Garlic, fresh basil, Parmesan, kale, mascarpone, potentially rosemary/thyme

Fresh
2 onions
1 bulb of garlic
Fresh basil
2 red onions
300 g kale
3-4 large aubergines
5 sprigs of rosemary
1 lemon
6 tomatoes
1 whole cucumber
1 iceburg lettuce
Fresh mint
750 g mushrooms
Fresh thyme (or could share rosemary)
50 g spring onions

Dairy
130 g Parmesan
250 g (2 balls mozzarella)
250 g Greek yoghurt
225 g mascarpone cheese

Meat & Seafood
500 g boneless, skinless chicken thighs
8 pork sausages
1.1 kg chicken thighs, skin on, on the bone

Pantry
2 x 500 g cartons passata
3 slices stale bread
7 tbsp nduja paste (1 jar)
400-500 g dried white beans
2 tubes tomato purée
1 x 400 g can plum tomatoes
375 g lasagne sheets
500 g fusilli

Cupboard Essentials
3 tbsp extra virgin olive oil
Dried oregano
3 tbsp rapeseed oil
Salt and pepper
Pinch of chilli flakes (optional)
250 g self-raising flour
2 vegetable stock cubes
½ tbsp olive oil

Meal Plan 5

- - - - - - - - - - - - -

5-ingredient Broccoli Mac 'n' Cheese
Page 130

Spicy Butter & Tomato White Fish with Vegetables
Page 107

Turkey Steaks with Peppercorn Sauce & Greens
Page 164

Cacio e Pepe Gnocchi
Page 163

Halloumi Curry
Page 100

Further Cost Savings
Substitute cherry tomato cans with chopped tomatoes if cheaper. Use hard cheese interchangeably with Parmesan.

Shared Ingredients
Garlic, butter, basil, single cream

Fresh
2 courgettes
1 red onion
1 bulb of garlic
Fresh basil
500 g leeks
2 onions
1 tbsp fresh ginger
150 g cavolo nero
1 large head of broccoli
½ lime
Fresh mint

Dairy
300 g extra-mature cheddar
50 g + 1 tbsp butter
300 ml single cream
100 g Parmesan
450 g (2 packs) low-fat halloumi

Meat & Seafood
4 turkey steaks (375 g)

Pantry
500 g macaroni
400 ml evaporated milk
2 x 400 g cans cherry tomatoes
1 kg (2 packs) of gnocchi
2 x 500 g cartons passata
350 g white rice

Cupboard Essentials
Salt and pepper
2 tbsp extra virgin olive oil
3 tbsp rapeseed oil
2 tbsp coarsely ground
 black pepper
2 becf stock cubes
2½ tbsp cornflour
1 tbsp curry powder
1 tbsp garam masala
1 tsp ground turmeric
Chilli flakes
1 tbsp Dijon mustard

Frozen
520 g frozen white fish fillets
200 g frozen peas

Index

Acknowledgements

There are so many amazing people that made my dream of writing a book a reality. But I have to start with my biggest supporter, who without their support I wouldn't have had the confidence to put recipes online – my amazing mum. You were just as enthusiastic as I was when I was brainstorming names on a napkin in a café back in 2018 and since then you have supported and helped me in so many ways, too many ways to write! You've helped me with ingredient runs, with shooting every day for this book (and even helped with the camera when I attempt to be a hand model), cleaning up together until midnight when our shoot days ran over. You even believed in the me enough to let me transform your spare bedroom into a studio, with all my equipment scattered around the house. I don't know what I would have done without your help with not only this book, but over the last four years of working on BTB. You're my number one supporter and I'll forever be grateful.

To my dad and brother Charlie. I'm so lucky to have the equivalent support from you. From head recipe tasters to clean up, taking on some of my admin, tech issues and brainstorming recipe ideas (Dad, I'm sorry that I haven't done your sausage and baked bean recipe yet – it's coming). If I ever have any issues, both of you are always ready to help as soon as I call and I can't thank you enough for that!

To the rest of my family – my cousins who comment on every post, my aunties who share my page with their friends and my grandma who likes every single story that I post, your support is unwavering and I'm so lucky to have the best family.

To my friends, we joke that everyone is part of the Beat the Budget team as it never feels like I'm working alone. You all hyped me up enough to brave getting in front of the camera when I wasn't confident enough to do it, you support every post and always try my recipes. There are too many of you to list but I have to mention Eve, Emma and Molly. Through every exciting stage of the book, I'm so thankful that you guys were by my side the whole time.

To Ross, thank you for being the calming influence when I was feeling overwhelmed or stressed. You reply to every recipe clip that I send you during the day with a different compliment each time and listen to me talking about food for hours on end. I'd share my noodles with you any day of the week. Thank you for everything!

To Sam, Alice, Dem and the rest of the team at Ebury, I can't believe how lucky I got with such an amazing team to make my dream book with. To Sam, for believing in me from day one when you reached out. You respond to my endless number of questions and have made this such a fun experience. Thank you for allowing me to bring my vision to life.

To my followers, I wouldn't be here without you. I still can't believe how much BTB has grown in the last year and without your trust in me in your kitchen, I wouldn't have been able to take the leap and work on Beat the Budget full time. Thank you for sticking with me on this journey and I hope that you'll love these recipes, as every idea is made with inspiration from comments, DMs and feedback that you provide. Thank you for everything.

Ebury Press an imprint of Ebury Publishing,
20 Vauxhall Bridge Road,
London SW1V 2SA

Ebury Press is part of the Penguin Random House group of companies
whose addresses can be found at global.penguinrandomhouse.com

Text © Mimi Harrison 2023
Photography & styling © Mimi Harrison 2023
except pages 7 and 239 © Dan Jones 2023

Mimi Harrison has asserted her right to be identified as the author of this
Work in accordance with the Copyright, Designs and Patents Act 1988

First published by Ebury Press in 2023

www.penguin.co.uk

A CIP catalogue record for this book is available from the British Library

ISBN 9781529908121

Design and Illustration: Beth Free, Studio Nic&Lou
Photography: Mimi Harrison & Dan Jones (pages 7 & 239)

Printed and bound in Italy by LEGO. SpA

The authorised representative in the EEA is Penguin Random House Ireland,
Morrison Chambers, 32 Nassau Street, Dublin D02 YH68.

Penguin Random House is committed to a sustainable future for our
business, our readers and our planet. This book is made from
Forest Stewardship Council® certified paper.